I HEAR MY SISTERS SAYING

I HEAR
MY SISTERS
SAYING

Poems by
Twentieth-Century Women

edited by Carol Konek
and Dorothy Walters

Thomas Y. Crowell Company
ESTABLISHED 1834   NEW YORK

Library of Congress Cataloging in Publication Data
Main entry under title:
I hear my sisters saying.
    1.   American poetry—Women authors.   2.   Ameri-
can poetry—20th century.   3.   Women—Poetry.
I.   Konek,   Carol.   II.   Walters,   Dorothy,   1928-
PS589.I2   811'.5'408   76-4973
ISBN 0-690-01107-5
ISBN 0-690-01092-3(pbk.)

   2   3   4   5   6   7   8   9   10

Introduction

Women today are deeply occupied with examining outworn notions of femininity, rejecting sanctified categories of female identity, and discovering—for themselves and the world—the New Woman so long announced and so late arriving. Nothing is more rewarding, ultimately, than discovery of self through the stripping away of surfaces to claim the deep reality within. The poems in this book are such a process, a piercing through to and embracing of truths too long buried or rejected. Each poem is, in its own way, both a protest and an affirmation.

I Hear My Sisters Saying traces the life experience of women as that experience is depicted in the poetry of the women of our age. There are poems of childhood, poems showing the roles of daughter and wife/lover, poems of disillusionment, of the conceiving of children and of poetry, of women in their relation to women, and of the madness bred by the conditions of modern society. Finally there are poems which suggest ways of bringing order into the chaos of existence.

Often the subjects themselves are commonplace: the familiar poles of birth and death and all that occupies the indeterminate human interval between. But the ways of looking at love in its many guises and at loss and the harsh recognitions it imposes are themselves special. Each work is charged with the special intensity of perception given to those occupied in that most important task of self-definition. Each vision records some fragment of the total experience of woman, whether of agony or rage or transcendence or despair. We believe that many women will recognize in these poems the features of their own experience, familiar stages in their own progress toward self-discovery.

Carol Konek and Dorothy Walters
WICHITA, KANSAS
October 1975

Contents

1

It took my childhood before I could see

the will's love

love God—
            my mother said
He who shut the Lion's mouth
and sealed the flames to their own burning

"the soul is like a little bird in His hand
a bird that lives in a wild briar tree"

love Life—my father said
laying the map out
            green-red mountains
            blue-yellow sea
the soul is a migrant
roe-bird that nests on sea rocks
a hawk   a falcon—
                        an eagle
or a "splatter-wing parrot
that only at night sleeps in a tree"

it took
my childhood before I could see

each one
said the same
            I am

                  love me

                        BESMILR BRIGHAM

Childhood

When I was a child I knew red miners
dressed raggedly and wearing carbide lamps.
I saw them come down red hills to their camps
dyed with red dust from old Ishkooda mines.
Night after night I met them on the roads,
or on the streets in town I caught their glance;
the swing of dinner buckets in their hands,
and grumbling undermining all their words.

I also lived in low cotton country
where moonlight hovered over ripe haystacks,
or stumps of trees, and croppers' rotting shacks
with famine, terror, flood, and plague near by;
where sentiment and hatred still held sway
and only bitter land was washed away.

MARGARET WALKER

The Girl in the Willow Tree

The girl in the willow tree is skipping church.
She has gone out to look

at her horse in the moonlight and climbed up
to the treehouse where she reads in the day.

She is taking off her clothes
in the glazed night of Texas summer, first
shirt, then jeans and pants

she is wondering why she has done this
and cannot answer the question truly

the horses move beautifully in the small pasture, nibbling
the bark from the young pear trees, later the trees will die

from this
but now the smooth light soaks the skin of the palomino
and the blue mare with the hole in her left nostril

and the girl is very happy, but not at ease.

Later, rising in the night to a child's cry,
the woman will remember and ask herself

and there will be no answer except the sudden
brightness of the light and cool skin, as if she had
   ventured
to touch herself.

CAROLYN MAISEL

Sunday Afternoon

After the First Communion
and the banquet of mangoes and
bridal cake, the young daughters
of the coffee merchant lay down
for a long siesta, and their white dresses
lay beside them in quietness
and the white veils floated
in their dreams as the flies buzzed.
But as the afternoon
burned to a close they rose
and ran about the neighborhood
among the halfbuilt villas
alive, alive, kicking a basketball, wearing
other new dresses, of bloodred velvet.

DENISE LEVERTOV

The Grace of
Cynthia's Maidenhood

He chants a boy-chant,
a whisper-chain
:   I heard that you heard that I said that I

                                            love

you
and a silverbird hovers,

shades the blush on her face,
the paling mouth;

and into her eyes
fall the shining feathers
of shyness and pleasure.

VINNIE-MARIE D'AMBROSIO

Spring

When I was
thirteen I
believed that
the mailman

had sperm on
his hands and
if he touched
me I would
be pregnant
if he brushed
against me
in the hall
from my pores would sprout twigs branches leaves
buds blossoms unfurling I'd be an apple
tree in my white wedding dress swelling
the room until flowers exploded into the street
and rose up filling the sky blowsy with
fruit to come

RUTH WHITMAN

Nikki-Rosa

childhood remembrances are always a drag
if you're Black
you always remember things like living in Woodlawn
with no inside toilet
and if you become famous or something
they never talk about how happy you were to have
your mother
all to yourself and
how good the water felt when you got your bath
from one of those
big tubs that folk in chicago barbecue in

and somehow when you talk about home
it never gets across how much you
understood their feelings
as the whole family attended meetings about Hollydale
and even though you remember
your biographers never understand
your father's pain as he sells his stock
and another dream goes
And though you're poor it isn't poverty that
concerns you
and though they fought a lot
it isn't your father's drinking that makes any difference
but only that everybody is together and you
and your sister have happy birthdays and very good
Christmasses
and I really hope no white person ever has cause
to write about me
because they never understand
Black love is Black wealth and they'll
probably talk about my hard childhood
and never understand that
all the while I was quite happy

NIKKI GIOVANNI

The Way It Is

I have always known
that had I been blonde
blue-eyed
with skin fabled white as the unicorn's

with cheeks tinted and pearled
as May morning on the lips of a rose
such commercial virtues
could never have led me to assume myself
anywhere near as beautiful as
my mother
whose willow fall of black hair
—now pirate silver—
I brushed as a child
(earning five cents)
when shaken free from the bun
as wrapped round and pinned
it billowed in a fine mist
from her proud shoulders
to her waist.

Brown as I am, she is browner.
Walnut
like the satin leaves of the oak
that fallen overwinter in woods
where night comes quickly
and whose wind-peaked piles
deepen the shadows of
such seizure.

Moreover, she is tall.
At her side standing
I feel I am still
that scarecrow child of
yesteryear:
owl-eyed
toothed, boned, and angled
opposite to her
soft southern presence—

an inaudible allegiance
but sweetening her attendance
upon strangers and friends.

Dark hair, dark skin
these are the dominant measures of
my sense of beauty
which explains possibly
why being a black girl
in a country of white strangers
I am so pleased with myself.

GLORIA ODEN

On Approaching My Birthday

My mother bore me in the heat of summer
when the grass blanched under sun's hammer stroke
and the birds sang off key, panting between notes,
and the pear trees once all winged with whiteness
sagged, breaking with fruit, and only the zinnias,
like harlots, bloomed out vulgar and audacious,
and when the cicadas played all day long
their hidden harpsichords accompanying
her grief, my mother bore me, as I say,
then died shortly thereafter, no doubt
of her disgust and left me her disease
when I grew up to wither into truth.

VASSAR MILLER

Mother

Mother, I may do violence to you:
Extract a group of proverbs from your flow
Of talk, punctuate your letters, renew
Your beauty from yellow photos that show
You happy. Or, again, I may blacken
Your prejudices, even sour your breath,
Describe in detail what did not happen
But in nightmare: myself strangled to death
By the life-stalk. I do not mean to bruise
Your sweet breasts with hard words. Forgive the child
In me that to construct its world must use
Prime matter, and on its own wall sees wild
Shapes. But not tonight, when curled on your feet
You read and doze, too real for me, too deep.

SHARON MAYER LIBERA

letter to my mother

I remember when a Sunday friend and I,
bored with the good words of the morning and
the pleasantries of the noon meal,
escaped to the vacant lot behind our house

to play in the tall goldenrod
and hidden in the top branches of the persimmon tree,
antagonize small children
unable to catch hold of the lower limbs.

How we teased obnoxious Stevie Bull,
spit on him with sing-song poems
and ripe orange persimmons
till he ran screaming through the weeds,
a rodent harassed by the jays,
into the nest of his old stone house.

How, seconds later, his mother
erupted through the screen door, arms flailing,
eyes ripping leaves from the top of the trees,
her voice frenzied and crackling
with promises of retribution
more immediate and terrible
than those threats of eternal damnation
we had absorbed nonchalantly a few hours before.
I still feel her words crash
through the soft sunlight,
shatter the colors of the warm afternoon
and scatter the laughter like dry leaves in a storm.

How I dropped hard to the ground,
my heart banging against my ears, bursting
through the last tangled minutes onto the front porch,
each stride bringing nearer the ring
of the phone,
each breath adding
new lines to my story.

I do not remember what she said when she called,

what I said in defense or what
you said at all
and though there will be no more
angry mothers, no more Sunday games,
no more teasing of innocence
sometimes in still moments
that autumn terror
returns
leaves me stunned,
breathless,
naked in the garden
and I hear the steady ringing of the phone
into the long night.

ANITA SKEEN

Foxfire

At eighty-six she takes to pressing flowers
   and carries a Manhattan directory, stained
with cosmos and moss roses. "They keep their hue.
   Yarrow is good. But daisies go yellow as
old gloves." Arranged in oval frames,
   the petals brown to moth wings. The glue
      doesn't show.

It's the Fourth of July and the kids
   want to swim. "All right. I go."
They swarm in the sun. They're all hers but she can
   hardly remember their names. "I'm five.

You asked me that before, Granny." "I'm Sharon." "No,
  he's David." "No, I'm Dan."
    She sits in her black suit,

too hot for July, in the fruity chintz
  chair, a scarab on roses. The boys
rage on the sand, bloated with lemonade.
  She watches her son unfold a cage like
an aviary, drop in the baby. Then far
  over the water they hear a parade
    and stand still, listening.

Nothing she hears. "Go and talk to Grandma."
  "Show us your book, Grandma, with the dead
flowers." She sees the drummers pass
  in their hot faces. The pages turn
and open a parlor, stuffed with hassocks,
  an organ with no works, birds under glass,
    and black umbrellas.

"Are you too warm, Mother?" But this man
  full of favors is not the boy she remembers,
who lives somewhere under glass, sleeping
  if she could find him among these children,
their hands blazing with foxglove and yarrow,
  if she could find herself, herself planting
    instead of keeping.

NANCY WILLARD

The Nude on the Bathroom Wall

I'll prop her, I swear, ankle, butt and chin
on the six free feet of wainscot and why not?
Godabove, it's the last place in the world
like the good old gone Victorian saloon

where a harried man can contemplate his soul
and the glories of womankind, those kind
if expensive women of parts, painted or real,
who live in the flesh. When my husband's

grandmother dies and goes to heaven sexless
I'll do it: paint him his very own lifesize
fictional self-portrait! He deserves no less
for surviving his yoked polarities.

Meantime, blind and deaf to everything but sin,
salvation tickles the tubes of her set:
Grandmaw always expected the worst, and waits
for desperately sensual bathers to drown.

GENA FORD

A Woman Mourned
by Daughters

Now, not a tear begun,
we sit here in your kitchen,
spent, you see, already.
You are swollen till you strain
this house and the whole sky.
You, whom we so often
succeeded in ignoring!
You are puffed up in death
like a corpse pulled from the sea;
we groan beneath your weight.
And yet you were a leaf,
a straw blown on the bed,
you had long since become
crisp as a dead insect.
What is it, if not you,
that settles on us now
like satin you pulled down
over our bridal heads?
What rises in our throats
like food you prodded in?
Nothing could be enough.
You breathe upon us now
through solid assertions
of yourself: teaspoons, goblets,
seas of carpet, a forest

of old plants to be watered,
an old man in an adjoining
room to be touched and fed.
And all this universe
dares us to lay a finger
anywhere, save exactly
as you would wish it done.

ADRIENNE RICH

Woman Skating

A lake sunken among
cedar and black spruce hills;
late afternoon.

On the ice a woman skating,
jacket sudden
red against the white,

concentrating on moving
in perfect circles.

(actually she is my mother, she is
over at the outdoor skating rink
near the cemetery. On three sides
of her there are streets of brown
brick houses; cars go by; on the
fourth side is the park building.
The snow banked around the rink

is grey with soot. She never skates
here. She's wearing a sweater and
faded maroon earmuffs, she has
taken off her gloves)

Now near the horizon
the enlarged pink sun swings down.
Soon it will be zero.

With arms wide the skater
turns, leaving her breath like a diver's
trail of bubbles.

Seeing the ice
as what it is, water:
seeing the months
as they are, the years
in sequence occurring
underfoot, watching
the miniature human
figure balanced on steel
needles (those compasses
floated in saucers) on time
sustained, above
time circling: miracle

Over all I place
a glass bell

MARGARET ATWOOD

The Question

Mother and listener she is, but she does not listen.
I look at her profile as I ask, the sweet blue-grey of eye
going obdurate to my youth as I ask the first grown
  sexual
question.   She cannot reply.
And from then on even past her death, I cannot fully
have language with my mother, not as daughter
and mother through all the maze and silences
of all the turnings.
Until my own child grows and asks, and until
I discover what appalled my mother long before,
  discover
who never delivered her, until their double weakness
  and
strength in myself
rouse and deliver me from that refusal.
I threw myself down on the pine-needle evening.
Although that old ancient poem never did come to me,
not from you, mother,
although in answer you did only panic, you did only
  grieve,
and I went silent alone, my cheek to the red pine-needle
earth, and although it has taken me all these years
and sunsets to come to you, past the dying, I know,
I come with my word alive.

MURIEL RUKEYSER

All the Dead Dears

In the Archaeological Museum in Cambridge is a stone
coffin of the fourth century A.D. containing the skele-
tons of a woman, a mouse and a shrew. The ankle-
bone of the woman has been slightly gnawn.

Rigged poker-stiff on her back
With a granite grin
This antique museum-cased lady
Lies, companioned by the gimcrack
Relics of a mouse and a shrew
That battened for a day on her ankle-bone.

These three, unmasked now, bear
Dry witness
To the gross eating game
We'd wink at if we didn't hear
Stars grinding, crumb by crumb,
Our own grist down to its bony face.

How they grip us through thin and thick,
These barnacle dead!
This lady here's no kin
Of mine, yet kin she is: she'll suck
Blood and whistle my marrow clean
To prove it. As I think now of her head,

From the mercury-backed glass
Mother, grandmother, greatgrandmother
Reach hag hands to haul me in,
And an image looms under the fishpond
    surface
Where the daft father went down
With orange duck-feet winnowing his
    hair—

All the long gone darlings: they
Get back, though, soon,
Soon: be it by wakes, weddings,
Childbirths or a family barbecue:
Any touch, taste, tang's
Fit for those outlaws to ride home on,

And to sanctuary: usurping the armchair
Between tick
And tack of the clock, until we go,
Each skulled-and-crossboned Gulliver
Riddled with ghosts, to lie
Deadlocked with them, taking root as
    cradles rock.

SYLVIA PLATH

Daring

Daddyboy
trickster hero
for whom
my heart became
a pulsating trampoline

who might
I have become
had you not been
an acrobat
whose amazing feats
of balance
and daring
kept my eyes
on a skyline
defined by your
doublebackflip

how might I
have kept my feet
on the ground
while you soared
higher
and higher
led my mind
reeling
upward

outward
my hope becoming
a pathetic net

still I long
to catch you
bring you down
to me

CAROL KONEK

The Beekeeper's Daughter

A garden of mouthings. Purple, scarlet-speckled,
        black
The great corollas dilate, peeling back their silks.
Their musk encroaches, circle after circle,
A well of scents almost too dense to breathe in.
Hieratical in your frock coat, maestro of the bees,
You move among the many-breasted hives,

My heart under your foot, sister of a stone.

Trumpet-throats open to the beaks of birds.
The Golden Rain Tree drips its powders down.
In these little boudoirs streaked with orange and red
The anthers nod their heads, potent as kings
To father dynasties. The air is rich.
Here is a queenship no mother can contest—

A fruit that's death to taste: dark flesh, dark parings.

In burrows narrow as a finger, solitary bees
Keep house among the grasses. Kneeling down
I set my eye to a hole-mouth and meet an eye.
Round, green, disconsolate as a tear.
Father, bridegroom, in this Easter egg
Under the coronal of sugar roses

The queen bee marries the winter of your year.

SYLVIA PLATH

Portrait of the Father

"To their young children, fathers are not wont to
unfold themselves entirely, Pierre. There are a
thousand and one odd little youthful peccadilloes, that
we think we may as well not divulge to them."
— HERMAN MELVILLE, *Pierre*

*(—But hasn't he always, anyway, cultivated
that air of mystery to make you think
that?)*

Once I stood in a green bough
of learning, decorating, in a
living room, the Christmas Tree
a few months before I
was myself to be married

& heard the incredible notion
that my father had been married
before he married my mother,
to a childish woman, he said,
wild & impetuous, it couldn't
last but a few months

    in those seconds of realization
of another whole relationship
for my father, which spilled new worlds
of sunshine meetings & fall leaf picnics
into my lap, he who was mature & routine
was not always so; mysterious liaisons
& coverlets crowded my mind

watching him carefully place
painted can lids & paper chains on
the Christmas tree, how like my gaze
at him to Pierre's musing stare at the
portrait of his rakish father
which he hung secretively, to get
it out of open light, in his closet

the jaunty air, caught in the portrait
as if he had just dropped in from visiting
the beautiful French girl; his buff vest,
the impetuous set of the dancing-figured
neckcloth,
        "Love's secrets, being mysteries,
ever pertain to the transcendent
& the infinite"

        O star, o Christmas Tree of
fifteen childhood christmases, O Father as Lover

(her and mine) in your own special world
of romance & mystery,
o infinite world of mysteries unfolding at the
hand of Fate whether we seek or not,
o world of the rainbow unknown &
moon world of the never but always possible
    to know,   prove to me that this life
I've been leading
has antecedents of more beautiful
mysterious nature, bells on hills ringing
I've heard only internally, in the back of
my invasive mind on quietest hilly nights in
moon-black verdure of summer . . .

LINDY HOUGH

a poem for my father

how sad it must be
to love so many women
to need so many black
perfumed bodies weeping
underneath you.
                    when i remember all those nights
i filled my mind with
long wars between short
sighted trojans & greeks
while you slapped some
wide hips about in
your pvt dungeon,

when i remember your
deformity   i want to
do something about your
makeshift manhood.
.i guess
           that is why
on meeting your sixth
wife, i cross myself
with her confessionals.

SONIA SANCHEZ

Legacy

Grandad, I didn't burn it, I
only wanted to. I never could
destroy the thing that hurts me:
I'm sending you my fiddle, you
wrote me, there's no one here
who can play it now.

And so it came, homely in its
varnished case and worn with
handling. (He was dying, the old
man, and I too far from dying
to forgive: the father who failed
us both, his father and child,

I would not beg of a last trip
home. He's not the son you

ever knew, I answered—even so,
the fiddle came. I gave it
to someone I wouldn't have to know.)
Do you understand now?

Long dead and beyond caring,
can you understand? There was
no one here who could play it.

GENA FORD

A Way of Keeping

This is the meadow of the mind.
Under that stone your father lies.
His lean horse tramples the withered grass
and thunder scatters the mourners' cries.
Among the graves your children pass,
hide crouching by strange stones to find
how every child's father dies
playing hard in the fierce beam
of summer wasting before your eyes
which see all creatures as they seem.

This is the forest of the heart.
Under that root your father sleeps.
Moles and hedgehogs, snails and stones
guard the cave where the children keep
their long watch over their father's bones.
On humps and horns, on wheels and carts,

satyrs and lizards and all that creeps
bind him in such a saving spell
worms pass him by and your spelled heart weeps
which sees all creatures as it will.

These are the waters of the soul,
a healing spring, wherein you find
never yourself but such far sight
hearts run aground and eyes go blind
to every creature they thought to hold,
and water spinning its holy light
gives back your father, simple, kind,
hymning the whole to praise the part:
the man in the meadow of the mind,
the god in the forest of the heart.

NANCY WILLARD

The Moss of His Skin

"Young girls in old Arabia were often buried alive next
to their dead fathers, apparently as sacrifice to the
goddesses of the tribes. . . ."
    —HAROLD FELDMAN, "Children of the Desert,"
Psychoanalysis and Psychoanalytic Review, Fall 1958

It was only important
to smile and hold still,
to lie down beside him

and to rest awhile,
to be folded up together
as if we were silk,
to sink from the eyes of mother
and not to talk.
The black room took us
like a cave or a mouth
or an indoor belly.
I held my breath
and daddy was there,
his thumbs, his fat skull,
his teeth, his hair growing
like a field or a shawl.
I lay by the moss
of his skin until
it grew strange. My sisters
will never know that I fall
out of myself and pretend
that Allah will not see
how I hold my daddy
like an old stone tree.

ANNE SEXTON

2

This man, this stranger in my arms

Indian Summer

This man, this stranger in my arms
Lies quiet now, below in sleep,
Lost in the deep seine of his dream.
How wide the net is cast, far out, far down,
But his dream plumbs himself; mine is my own.

Two feral figures in the jungle half-
Light taut in struggle
Shoulder to shoulder,
Cold hate, colder force
In the leashed clash of wrestlers
Clasped in war in
One another's arms;
There they enact
The ancient drama of possession.
But who has won?
Deep down within the womb
Of dream, of his own dream,
Each acts his part, and is by it possessed.

Time's horn of plenty spills
Out to us her dialectic
Changing forms;
No one can say
When love will take root,
Run wildfire up the heart's trellis. We
Harbor such diversity

That turning now we find
The future in our arms,
A golden cataract that comes
Out of the cornucopia of dream.

BARBARA HOWES

And This Is Love

And this is love: two souls
That freely meet, and have
No need of proving anything;

No need of grasping, holding,
Forcing, and no need
Of needing: love is all.

It never can be satisfied,
Nor would it want to be—
Such love knows better than
To end itself. To satisfy
Would end it: let it be!

Then let us freely play
With all we have. Can lips
Kiss more than eyes? Two
Voices rise: could bodies mingle more?

This love brings harmonies
That fill the air:

We meet to celebrate,
And everything we do is love.

Paula Reingold

Alive Together

Speaking of marvels, I am alive
together with you, when I might have been
alive with anyone under the sun,
when I might have been Abelard's woman
or the whore of a Renaissance pope
or a peasant wife with not enough food
and not enough love, with my children
dead of the plague. I might have slept
in an alcove next to the man
with the golden nose, who poked it
into the business of stars
or sewn a starry flag
for a general with wooden teeth.
I might have been the exemplary Pocahontas
or a woman without a name
weeping in Master's bed
for my husband, exchanged for a mule,
my daughter, lost in a drunken bet,
I might have been stretched on a totem pole
to appease a vindictive god
or left, a useless girl-child,
to die on a cliff. I like to think
I might have been Mary Shelley

in love with a wrong-headed angel,
or Mary's friend. I might have been you.
This poem is endless, the odds against us are endless,
the chances of being alive together
statistically non-existent;
still we have made it, alive in a time
when rationalists in square hats
and hatless Jehovah's Witnesses
agree it is almost over,
alive with our lively children
who, but for endless ifs,
would have missed out on being alive
together with marvels and follies
and longings and lies and wishes
and error and humor and mercy
and journeys and voices and faces
and colors and summers and mornings
and knowledge and tears and chance.

LISEL MUELLER

28 VIII 69

leaving them, running
through rice hail,
my mother breaks from the edge
of the crowd
like heat lightning, her hands
upon my shoulders,
that yellow coil of light before a summer storm,

granma her thin arms tucking
sweet ears of corn and hope;
Jill her hot dark hair
ringed with blue and yellow flowers
beside the car, the motor ready,
window open receiving rain—
Cynthia finds it; I bend to her
my sister. she tells me now with arms
her toast, where the night before
with soft face bowed
her hands clutched in the feelings;
she could not say.
they lent me flight of strength
in close departing;
and it is hailing now
at once with melting in my throat,
seeing four sunbirds flashing
through a storm.

geoffrey you have given me
a lake for a heart
where we slide through at night
unaware that it is water keeping us
afloat; you have given me your name
a blue bath towel, opening like a morning glory
then wrapping us together

LAURA CHESTER

The Marriage Wig

*"If you're going to marry, make sure you first know whom
you're going to divorce."*

—Yiddish proverb

1.

The Mishnah says I blind you with my hair,
that when I bind it in a net
my fingers waylay my friends;
that in a close house I shake loose
the Pleiades into your kitchen.

How can I let you see me, past and future,
blemishes and dust? Must I
shear away my hair and wear
the wig the wisemen say? Will you
receive me, rejoice me, take me for your wall?

To any man not blind, a wig is false.

2.

Once upon a time I wrote a boy
into my calendar of weddings. We lived
in a gargoyle house with many eyes.
Snow furred the street lamps. Inside
we had our wine, one pot, an innocent fire.

Now the gargoyle house is gone. On a tree
is the orphan number, forty-nine, meaning
49, a house, a marriage, a time
scythed clean, crunched to powder, flat
as a grave, as though we'd never been.

Let me apologize for that lost number.

3.
Let me apologize for all the faces
I've worn, none of them my own.
See me in my glass. A ghost looks back,
a witty ghost, who counterfeits my mask,
wearing a marriage wig made of my hair.

Inside, I'm threaded on a passion
taut as a tightrope. Strip away the hair,
the tooth, the wrinkle, the obscene
cartoon that decades scrawl—
underneath I'm naked as a nun.

I wear that nakedness for a disguise.

RUTH WHITMAN

41

Ghost Poem Five

lovers who
came to me
brought words
arms full of words
whole portmanteaux
lay with us
making cover to the long
discovery of touch

and you   the lover
bring silence to my bed
shadowed   speechless
you beckon never sound
your cry
the one for whom my tears
are blood   are bones
to make my body full
and moonless light

MARY NORBERT KÖRTE

To the Man I Live With

On the other side
of my world
I write poems,
love my poets
and the wine we share.
(you never go there)
But I must pass
where you are
going either way.
Sometimes I fear
losing one world
for the other.
I have no choice.
I offer love to both.

ANN MENEBROKER

So We've Come at Last
to Freud

Do not hold my few years
                            against me
In my life, childhood
                        was a myth
So long ago it seemed, even
                              in the cradle.

Don't label my love with slogans;
My father can't be blamed
                          for my affection
Or lack of it;
ask him.
He won't understand you.

Don't sit on holy stones
                       as you,
Loving me
            and hating me, condemn.
There is no need for that.

I like to think that I, though
                        young it's true,
Know what
           I'm doing.

That I, once unhappy, am
Now
Quite sanely
                    jubilant,
& that neither you
Nor I can
Deny
That no matter how
"Sick"
The basis
is
Of what we have,
What we *do* have
Is Good.

ALICE WALKER

In Spite of His Dangling Pronoun

He was really her favorite
student dark and just
back from the army with
hot olive eyes, telling her of
bars and the first
time he got a piece of
ass in Greece or was it
Italy and drunk on some strange
wine and she thought
in spite of his dangling
pronoun (being twenty four and

never screwed but in her
soft nougat thighs) that he
would be a
lovely experience.
So she shaved her legs up high
and when he came
talking of footnotes she
locked him tight in her
snug black file cabinet where
she fed him twice a day and
hardly anyone noticed
how they lived among bluebooks
in the windowless office
rarely coming up for sun or the
change in his pronoun or the
rusty creaking chair
or that many years later
they were still going to town in
novels she never had time to finish

LYN LIFSHIN

A Family Man

We are talking in bed. You show me snapshots.
Your wallet opens like a salesman's case
on a dog, a frame house hung with shutters
and your eyes reset in a child's face.
Here is your mother standing in full sun
on the veranda back home. She is wearing

what we used to call a washdress. Geraniums
flank her as pious in their bearing
as the soap and water she called down on your head.
We carry around our mothers. But mine is dead.

Out of the celluloid album, cleverly as a shill
you pull an old snap of yourself squatting beside
a stag you shot early in the war in the Black Hills.
The dog tags dangle on your naked chest.
The rifle, broken, lies across your knees.
What do I say to the killer you love best,
that boy-man full of his summer expertise?
I with no place in the file will
wake on dark mornings alone with him in my head.
This is what comes of snapshots. Of talking in bed.

MAXINE KUMIN

Moon as Medusa

Such easy, easy hours
when their porch has started fading
into a long and dark and middle gulf—

his mouth and mine brushing and rubbing
and freshening
and parting, O's joining and
dropping
and swelling small and
adhering and brushing

in long and easy creations: those mouth rounds and
ovals, those slow brims arching,
the mouth-curves like four acrobats
in a drowsing circus
bending over and over, partners
of touching-shapes—pears, hearts, wreaths—
until at once only one flesh-ring lives,
a lamp of lips,
a knowing dayglow valve;

and our legs and arms and torsos
are undressed
furniture,
distant,
like the mattress's abysses and
the flimsying rugs and the pulverizing
soundless windows;

as if all—bedroom and body-extensions—
have begged to be excused,
and thinned down,
and gone outside to the elm, itself
perforating into night,
or farther out to the moon's flying wane,
or vanished over the skies' aisles:

all in a passion of exit
so low-keyed and un-insistent
that the lips never notice in the
lit concentration
on their own easy hours;

but always something (it was
the moon once when

48

clouds like snakes' mouths
were falling around her mowing jaw)
some Medusa-fury
fires the edge of the elm
and then the grainy window,
and under the shower of light
the lips' shadows
dance a
turnabout
in the thickening room.

VINNIE-MARIE D'AMBROSIO

The Blind Leading the Blind

Take my hand. There are two of us in this cave.
The sound you hear is water; you will hear it forever.
The ground you walk on is rock. I have been here before.
People come here to be born, to discover, to kiss,
to dream and to dig and to kill. Watch for the mud.
Summer blows in with scent of horses and roses;
fall with the sound of sound breaking; winter shoves
its empty sleeve down the dark of your throat.
You will learn toads from diamonds, the fist from the
    palm,
love from the sweat of love, falling from flying.
There are a thousand turnoffs. I have been here before.
Once I fell off a precipice. Once I found gold.
Once I stumbled on murder, the thin parts of a girl.
Walk on, keep walking, there are axes above us.

Watch for occasional bits and bubbles of light—
birthdays for you, recognitions: *yourself, another.*
Watch for the mud. Listen for bells, for beggars.
Something with wings went crazy against my chest once.
There are two of us here. Touch me.

LISEL MUELLER

Growing Together

we have tangled together
too often
our sleep has tangled mossy and sinister
as old rocks
our faces pressed together in sleep
have taken on the slumber of rocks, rocks' faces,
which are the least important part
of rocks

the veins of your forehead have swollen
like vines
my hair has grown too long
down onto your chest
our toenails outlined in harmless old dirt
scrape against all our legs
for weeks

we have embraced
too often
our arms have tangled slick with sweat

like the sweat of oil on water
making phosphorescent
the swimmers and their innocent limbs
the glow shows them everywhere
no escape in any dark

rising, pulling back my long sweaty hair
I see a face in the mirror only half mine
what I am thinking is only half mine
these words are only half mine
the frayed threads of our bodies want
only that tangling again
that old growing together again
a completion like the exhaling
of a single breath

JOYCE CAROL OATES

Bedtime

We are a meadow where the bees hum,
mind and body are almost one

as the fire snaps in the stove
and our eyes close,

and mouth to mouth, the covers
pulled over our shoulders,

we drowse as horses drowse afield,
in accord; though the fall cold

surrounds our warm bed, and though
by day we are singular and often lonely.

DENISE LEVERTOV

. . . The Dancer from the Dance

We are lovers
after our fashion,
ten years married
and alone for one night.

In the midnight dark
the lamps are out,
the airconditioner rattles
behind drawn drapes.
On an unfamiliar bed
we drink wine
we make love.

At home in the country
our children surely sleep
and will not disturb us
with cries from tigery dreams.
Tonight we are free
to our own devices.

We are such old friends
our bodies yield no surprises
in this hotel evening

above the muted traffic;
but pleasure from touching,
holding, moving together
still complements the cool sensation
of wine on the tongue.

It is that same dance
we've always done
(the one that brought applause
at Christmas parties, weddings):
fingers, lips, legs, tongue
all know the choreography.
On a bed suspended in the city sky,
with Lautrec ballerinas
keeping time in their frames,
we move to music cherished
but predictable:

the finale is always the same.

SUZANNE JUHASZ

To a Husband

Your voice at times a fist
        Tight in your throat
Jabs ceaselessly at phantoms
        In the room,
Your hand a carved and
        skimming boat

Goes down the Nile
        To point out Pharaoh's tomb.

You're Africa to me
        At brightest dawn.
The Congo's green and
        Copper's brackish hue,
A continent to build
        With Black Man's brawn.
I sit at home and see it all
        Through you.

                        MAYA ANGELOU

Extensions of Linear Mobility

We marry our grandfathers
and theirs and beyond:
all the people who settle
and unsettle our past
and offer us more than our life.

Early in foreplay
the letterless nameless ones
nestled in memories
reach out for revival
and approach the familiar.

A quick penetration and X meets Y
in a gypsy camp; their son W

rustles ponies in Scotland.
M and O throw darts
as L brings more whiskey
and A through K cheer them all.
The rest of the lettered
build fires or fences,
run trains or make music,
own salons or guns
or vineyards or gods.

Closer to climax
your grandfather the puddler
from Stockton-on-Tees
shares a stout with my Granny
old hooker from Bonn.
Genteel Aunt Mary serves tea to Albert
whose soul still belongs
to Metropolitan Life.
Florence and Joker decide to go fishing,
throw lines for the names
that flash to the surface.

We pull up the blankets
on spent generations.

JEANINE HATHAWAY

3

I am trying to think how a woman can be a rock

No More Soft Talk

Don't ask a geologist about rocks.
Ask me.

That man,
he said.

What can you do with him?
About him?
He's a rock.

No, not a rock,
I said.
  Well,
a very brittle rock, then.
One that crumbles easily, then.
Is crushed to dust, finally.

Me.
I said.
I am the rock.
The hard rock.
You can't break me.

I am trying to think how a woman
can be a rock,
when all she wants is to be soft,
to melt to the lines
her man draws for her.

But talking about rocks
intelligently
must be
talking about different kinds
of rock.

What happens to the brain
in shock? Is it
like an explosion
of flowers and blood,
staining the inside
of the skull?

I went to my house,
to see my man,
found the door locked,
and something I didn't plan
on—a closed bedroom door
(my bed)
another woman's handbag on the couch.
Is someone in the bedroom?

Yes, Yes,
a bed full of snakes all bearing new young,
a bed of slashed wrists,
a bed of carbines and rifles with no ammunition,
a bed of my teeth in another woman's fingers.

Then the answer to rocks,
as I sit here and talk.

The image of an explosion:
a volcanic mountain
on a deserted pacific island.

What comes up,
like gall in my throat,
a river of abandoned tonsils that can no longer cry,
a sea of gold wedding rings and smashed glasses,
the lava, the crushed and melted rock
comes pouring out now,
down this mountain you've never seen,
from this face that believed in you,
rocks that have turned soft,
but now are bubbling out of the lips of a mountain,
into the ocean raising the temperature
to 120 degrees.
If your ship were here
it would melt all the caulking.

This lava,
hot and soft,
will cool someday,
and turn back into the various stones.
None of it is
my rock.
My rock doesn't crumble.
My rock is the mountain.
Love me
if you can.
I will not make it easy for you
anymore.

DIANE WAKOSKI

Even There

it was December
and yes finally
you wanted me
we ran down the
slick narrow road
houses leaned
together the colors
wine and brown
remember the cracked
snow our scarves
floating getting
there out of
breath our
hair melting
boots clicked under
the door there
were quilts on the
sloped ceiling
and the old
stove you smiled
toward going to
heat up some
coffee. I kept
looking around
to get it right:
your suede jacket
hanging in several

places your
mouth was
corduroy I wanted
to touch
but even in the
dream every
time I came
close to you
the place that
was you
changed to air

LYN LIFSHIN

They Went Home

They went home and told their wives,
   that never once in all their lives,
   had they known a girl like me,
But . . . They went home.

They said my house was licking clean,
   no word I spoke was ever mean,
   I had an air of mystery,
But . . . They went home.

My praises were on all men's lips,
   they liked my smile, my wit, my hips,
   they'd spend one night, or two or three.
But . . .

MAYA ANGELOU

For My Lover,
Returning to His Wife

She is all there.
She was melted carefully down for you
and cast up from your childhood,
cast up from your one hundred favorite aggies.

She has always been there, my darling.
She is, in fact, exquisite.
Fireworks in the dull middle of February
and as real as a cast-iron pot.

Let's face it, I have been momentary.
A luxury. A bright red sloop in the harbor.
My hair rising like smoke from the car window.
Littleneck clams out of season.

She is more than that. She is your have to have,
has grown you your practical your tropical growth.
This is not an experiment. She is all harmony.
She sees to oars and oarlocks for the dinghy,

has placed wild flowers at the window at breakfast,
sat by the potter's wheel at midday,
set forth three children under the moon,
three cherubs drawn by Michelangelo,

done this with her legs spread out
in the terrible months in the chapel.
If you glance up, the children are there
like delicate balloons resting on the ceiling.

She has also carried each one down the hall
after supper, their heads privately bent,
two legs protesting, person to person,
her face flushed with a song and their little sleep.

I give you back your heart.
I give you permission—

for the fuse inside her, throbbing
angrily in the dirt, for the bitch in her
and the burying of her wound—
for the burying of her small red wound alive—

for the pale flickering flare under her ribs,
for the drunken sailor who waits in her left pulse,
for the mother's knee, for the stockings,
for the garter belt, for the call—

the curious call
when you will burrow in arms and breasts
and tug at the orange ribbon in her hair
and answer the call, the curious call.

She is so naked and singular.
She is the sum of yourself and your dream.
Climb her like a monument, step after step.
She is solid.

As for me, I am a watercolor.
I wash off.

ANNE SEXTON

The Paisley Ceiling

Looking up
I find myself written
in design language
smiles with a curious
twist at one corner,
tears with curved tails,
chalk-white phalluses
with raspberry ticklers

apricot vaginas
opening like tulips
rolled french horns
of rose and gold
singing tones the
shape of pears turning:
all seduce more of me
daily, hourly.

Finally when
I can't be found
down in worn footprints
by the undreaming sink
paring parsnips
raging at radishes
feeding my soul
inadequate peaches

I, become Paisley,
will be up there
where your tweed eyes
can never trace
the lines of my face
concealed like an object
in a child's puzzle
disguised as chimney stone.

Loving your honest
Harrisness
I swam in herringbone
seas to please you,
neither fish nor amphibian
as you truly are.
But I have floundered
to my last near-drowning.

So bring another woman
in. Let her be of
hand-loomed twill
textured by shrinking
colored by dying
to shades of heather;
let her hum
in grayest weather

a tweedling song
as she seeds fruit
or feeds your soul
tinned adequate peaches
or kneads the bread;
let her tears be tweed
when peeling old onions.

I will be watching

a bright dry eye
a coral paisley cobra.

LILA ARNOLD

I Wake, My Friend, I

wake. and my eyes stun
you. and my voice shakes
you. i wake. and look
for you, look at
you. and you think i am an enormous plant, a
    carnivorous plant
come to lick you off the surface of your life.
and i am.
and i will. you

shake at the thought that i
am free to walk as my own
shape. to move
my feet free from the pot
theyve been buried in. they are
free. see, i

walk. i walk. and you think
i am knives and revolvers. you think i am war and
    murder.
and i am, my friend, i

am. and you think i make judgments
on your small, dark life. and i do, my friend, i do.
and you
sit. and you
sit. and you hear
movement. the carpet. the wall tack. the sheet. and you
blink your eyes.
and your mouth wont shut.
and you wag it.
and you wag it.
and i

glow like a comet rising in the sky. and i
gnash my teeth. and i am painted blue
and orange. and i jump
the way fire jumps. and i am explosions and steel. and i
am soft meat. and i am buttons and silver. and i am
books and thread. and i am tongues
and laughter. and i am tin
and singing. and

electricity is the way i touch. and
night is the way i bend
my legs. and my hair, my hair revolves
the sun. and i

knock at your door. and i
am feathers and claws. rings and knuckles.
i dance. i laugh. and you think
ive come to kiss holes in your gauze
face. and your throat
is a closet. and your ears are wrapped in phlegm. and
    your fingers
hang useless. and you think

you wont hear me, you think
you wont touch me. but you will, my friend, you
will.

FAYE KICKNOSWAY

Living in Sin

She had thought the studio would keep itself;
no dust upon the furniture of love.
Half heresy, to wish the taps less vocal,
the panes relieved of grime. A plate of pears,
a piano with a Persian shawl, a cat
stalking the picturesque amusing mouse
had risen at his urging.
Not that at five each separate stair would writhe
under the milkman's tramp; that morning light
so coldly would delineate the scraps
of last night's cheese and three sepulchral bottles;
that on the kitchen shelf among the saucers
a pair of beetle-eyes would fix her own—
envoy from some village in the moldings . . .
Meanwhile, he, with a yawn
sounded a dozen notes upon the keyboard,
declared it out of tune, shrugged at the mirror,
rubbed at his beard, went out for cigarettes;
while she, jeered by the minor demons,
pulled back the sheets and made the bed and found
a towel to dust the table-top,
and let the coffee-pot boil over on the stove.

By evening she was back in love again,
though not so wholly but throughout the night
she woke sometimes to feel the daylight coming
like a relentless milkman up the stairs.

ADRIENNE RICH

Journey

Traveling for days to reach you,
my mind—a room full of telephones ringing
and no one to answer them; hundreds of phones ringing
in an empty room—
I cannot stop to relax. At night I am traveling,
transfering from one train to another. During the day
I am walking from one end of the train
to the other; in order to be nearer the right end
of the station when I must transfer
to another train—
always at a different end—the coming and going.

How many times have I packed and unpacked the bag
not knowing what items I would have to declare at the
    border
of each country? Finally, I have thrown everything away
but the bag of oranges to suck
and a gold bracelet you gave me with a running horse
on it, a charm. "Where am I going," I ask,
but my ticket has another hundred unmarked stations on
    it.

And you bought the ticket, so it must go to the right
    place—
a hundred stations to transfer.
Now I am not sure what I will find when I reach my
    destination.
You have shifted—or my feelings have—
in all the transfering, from train to train. I cannot be sure
which direction is North, never seeing trees anymore
to determine what side of the trunk moss grows on.

Perhaps when I get there, I will find
a room full of phones ringing; and no one to answer
    them.
Hundreds of phones ringing in a empty room.
This morning I lost the gold charm off my bracelet—
I must have dropped it when transfering.

D<small>IANE</small> W<small>AKOSKI</small>

The Mutes

Those groans men use
passing a woman on the street
or on the steps of the subway

to tell her she is a female
and their flesh knows it,

are they a sort of tune,
an ugly enough song, sung
by a bird with a slit tongue

but meant for music?

Or are they the muffled roaring
of deafmutes trapped in a building that is
slowly filling with smoke?

Perhaps both.

Such men most often
look as if groan were all they could do,
yet a woman, in spite of herself,

knows it's a tribute:
if she were lacking all grace
they'd pass her in silence:

so it's not only to say she's
a warm hole. It's a word

in grief-language, nothing to do with
primitive, not an ur-language;
language stricken, sickened, cast down

in decrepitude. She wants to
throw the tribute away, dis-
gusted, and can't,

it goes on buzzing in her ear,
it changes the pace of her walk,
the torn posters in echoing corridors

spell it out, it
quakes and gnashes as the train comes in.
Her pulse sullenly

had picked up speed,
but the cars slow down and
jar to a stop while her understanding

keeps on translating:
"Life after life after life goes by.

without poetry,
without seemliness,
without love."

DENISE LEVERTOV

Finding You

1.
Maybe it was the way
I was awakened this dawn,
a fire pouring out of my wrist,
that made me get up and look for you.
Heaven knows where you have been
or where you go at nights. I can only see
the stars burning up
the soles of your feet.

2.
If I could say yes,
yes, I understand. All kinds
of people I know leave their houses
at such odd hours gathering stones,
lumps of earth, small green roots.

I would leash you by your necktie
to my throat if I thought it
would do any good.

3.

How can I bring you back, anyhow?
I have cracked my feet, dissected
my tongue, pulled off my skin. I have
punched my way through stacks of hay
tented in fields in the October wind,
pulled at the cattails in the marshlands
behind the river, chopped off the ice
thickening on the trees. You are
never any of these.

4.

Maybe you should know I have moved
the bed next to the window.

5.

I hope you realize
I need your terrible
good-byes. It gives me something
to look forward to.

VIRGINIA GILBERT

Outside

grotesque, the line of trees, pronged
branches through the fog: the low cloud
passing, granular
& self-involved.

stare out the window. don't.
their life is theirs
this one
our own.

a closed cold room. possessions.
shelves of silent words, the anger
silting down. our life
together.

back.
come back
there isn't any
where to go.

PHYLLIS BEAUVAIS

The Fertile Valley of the Nile

In ancient Egypt,
where so many famous queens reigned,
a few were distinguished for their humane rule:
not a man was denied merely because of his sex.

Others,
unladylike perhaps,
and prejudiced no doubt by the deep-entrenched mode
mocked their catless gait,
poked fun at needle-fumbling thumbs,
at gruff voices against the gut-strung lute.
(It would have been too obviously cruel
to laugh at their lack of funds.)

Many
graciously adopted husbands into their own abodes;
saying, "Consider this your home even as it is mine.

"And,
if the time should arrive when I desire you to leave—
allay your fears,
I intend to settle
a good round womanly sum
upon the bony scruff of your departing neck."

EVE MERRIAM

The Key to Everything

Is there anything I can do
or has everything been done
or do
you prefer somebody else to do
it or don't
you trust me to do
it right or is it hopeless and no one can do
a thing or do
you suppose I don't
really want to do
it and am just saying that or don't
you hear me at all or what?

You're
waiting for
the right person the doctor or
the nurse the father or
the mother or
the person with the name you keep
mumbling in your sleep
that no one ever heard of there's no one
named that really
except yourself maybe

If I knew what the name was I'd
prove it's your own name
twisted in some way the one you

keep mumbling but you
won't tell me your
name or
don't you know it
yourself that's it
of course you've
forgotten or
never quite knew it or
weren't willing to believe it

Then there *is* something I
can do I
can find your name for you
that's the key to everything once you'd
repeat it clearly you'd
come awake you'd
get up and walk knowing where you're
going where you
came from

And you'd
love me
after that or would you
hate me?
no once you'd
get there you'd
remember and love me
of course I'd
be gone by then I'd
be far away

MAY SWENSON

Harbor

I catch myself drifting
toward you yet.
When I am tired, hours seem to be lifting
me into an old harbor. I forget

the tide is out now, foam breaking
on reefs; on black water, the hissing shelf
of the last wave shoreward, waking,
I catch myself.

NANCY PRICE

The Masochist

My black-eyed lover broke my back,
that hinge I swung on in and out
and never once thought twice about,

expecting a lifetime guarantee.
He snapped that simple hinge for me.
My black-eyed lover broke my back.

All delicate with touch and praise

he one by one undid the screws
that held the pin inside its cup

and when I toppled like a door
—his bitch, his bountiful, his whore—
he did not stay to lift me up.

Beware of black-eyed lovers. Some
who tease to see you all undone,
who taste and take you in the game

will later trample on your spine
as if they never called you *mine*,
mine, mine.

MAXINE KUMIN

Fire Island

The sea is obsidian
The sea is jade
The sea is a thousand Iroquois arrowheads
Piercing the shore.
My body is borne over the sea
I move on the backs of fishes
Swimming toward an island of cannibals
Ravenous for large, juicy genitals.
My body rises and my body falls
Listing toward the open air asylum,
Where I, as a woman

Shall walk on the bones of men
Ignoring the sacramental siphoned skull
Whose capped and sterile teeth
Whisper the great lie, "Love."

RITA MAE BROWN

sequence for a young widow passing

the yellow chrysanthemums
disturb me
my heart is a golden bowl

. . . .

the young widow's pain
is quite bright:
she glimmers
where she sits still-handed

the young widow
hesitates at the door
starts
            at the touch of green

with what white hands
she gathers pale leaves
caught between brittle stone

she waited for spring

the touch of breaking ice
anticipated her

sprinkling cuttings
of sandalwood leaves,
she makes her way to the river

. . . .

night. i
huddle by a lantern
there is but the sound of crickets

february
my lids are weighted, moons
ride heavy in the hills

memory:
            a lotus sails
the black river
much like a sleeping hand

sable brush, a potter's
bottle of ink—
where are the letters to go?

six hundred reasons
but three pines
collect my thoughts, my undone hair

red leaves, and in my heart
o what nights the gathering
of red moonlight

. . . .

potter's crucible
filled with parsley
blanched almonds and sweet
burnt laughter

among the poppy
a woman strays her
lotus hands stained red

she stares at birds
passage in dusky v's
her hands feathering her side

whenever it rains
the young widow laughs
the pools at her feet are red

. . . .

when at last they opened her
breast, no one dared touch
that red pulsing star

DEBORAH MUNRO

To Be in Love

To be in love
Is to touch things with a lighter hand.

In yourself you stretch, you are well.

You look at things
Through his eyes.
   A Cardinal is red.
   A sky is blue.
Suddenly you know he knows too.
He is not there but
You know you are tasting together
The winter, or light spring weather.

His hand to take your hand is overmuch.
Too much to bear.

You cannot look in his eyes
Because your pulse must not say
What must not be said.

When he
Shuts a door—
Is not there—
Your arms are water.

And you are free
With a ghastly freedom.

You are the beautiful half
Of a golden hurt.

You remember and covet his mouth,
To touch, to whisper on.

Oh when to declare
Is certain Death!

Oh when to apprize
Is to mesmerize.

To see fall down, the Column of Gold,
Into the commonest ash.

GWENDOLYN BROOKS

The Weather of Six Mornings

1.

Sunlight lies along my table
like abandoned pages.

I try to speak
of what is so hard for me—

this clutter of a life—
puritanical signature!

In the prolonged heat
  insects,
pine needles, birch leaves

make a ground bass of
  silence
that never quite dies.

2.

Treetops are shuddering
in uneasy clusters

like rocking water

whirlpooled before a
    storm.

Words knock at my breast,
heave and struggle to get
    out.

A black-capped bird
pecks on, unafraid.

Yield then, yield
to the invading rustle of
    the rain.

    3.
All is closed in
by an air so rain-drenched

the distant barking of tied-
    up dogs
ripples to the heart of the
    woods.

Only a man's voice
refuses to be absorbed.

Hearing of your death
by a distant roadside

I wanted to erect some
    marker
though your ashes float out
    to sea.

4.

If the weather breaks
I can speak of your dying,

if the weather breaks,
if the crows stop calling

and flying low
(again today there is
   thunder

outlying. . . .),
I can speak of your living,

the lightning-flash of
   meeting,
the green leaves waving at
   our windows.

5.

Yesterday a letter
spoke of our parting—

a kind of dissolution
so unlike this sudden
   stoppage.

Now all the years in
   between
flutter away like lost
   poems.

And the morning light is so
   delicate,
so utterly empty. . . .

at high altitude, after long
   illness,
breathing in mote by mote
   a vanished world. . . .

      6.
Rest.
A violin bow, a breeze

just touches the birches.
Cheep—a new flute

tunes up in a birch top.
A   chipmunk's   warning
   skirrs. . . .

Whose foot disturbs these
   twigs?
To the sea of received
   silence

why should I sign
my name?

JANE COOPER

4
What have I made

The Children

What have I made
children
with voices like bull-calves bellowing
tall like the legendary children of the tribes
of the California
earth-children
to make friends with the burrowing moles
grass—
children sprouting everywhere (seeded
on impossible wings) wild
weed-children
                    wood—
children
saplings all bark and twigs
air-children flying
children in the spring
where it bubbles up without let-up
slow sleepy children
heavy-lidded
nodding
in sun in shade
hot cold wet dry soft hard
tadpoles with see-through tails
naked nestlings
blind nurslings
sly

greedy
Oh, bite, teeth!
Kick, feet!
Pinch! Punch! (Pow!
Bam!! Blam!! Zap!!) AlL
                                    O
                                      V
                                        E
                                          R

made
love made
children

CONSTANCE URDANG

Poems for the New

1.

we're connecting,
            foot under my rib.
I'm sore with life!
At night,
            your toes grow. Inches of the new!
The lion prowls the sky
and shakes his tail for you.
Pieces of moon
            fly by my kitchen window.
And your father comes
riding the lion's back

                    in the dark,
to hold me,
                you,
                    in the perfect circle of him.

    2.

Voluptuous against him, I am
nothing superfluous,
but all—
bones, bark of him, root of him take.
I am round
with his sprouting,
new thing new thing!
He wraps me.
The sheets are white.
My belly has tracks on it—
                    hands and feet
are moving
under this taut skin.
In snow, in light,
we are about to become!

KATHLEEN FRASER

Poem Wondering if I'm Pregnant

Is it you? Are you there,
thief I can't see,
        drinking,
            leaving me at the edge

of breathing?
New mystery floating up my left arm,
clinging to the curtain.
        Uncontrollable.
Eyes on stalks, full of pollen,
stem juice, petals making ready to unfold,
to be set in a white window,
or an empty courtyard.
Fingers fresh. And cranium,
        a clean architecture
        with doors
        that swing open . . .
is it you, penny face?
Is it you?

KATHLEEN FRASER

Foetal Song

The vehicle gives a lurch but seems
to know its destination.
In here, antique darkness. I guess at things.
Tremors of muscles communicate
secrets to me. I am nourished.
A surge of blood pounding sweet
blossoms my gentle head.
I am perfumed wax melted of holy candles
I am ready to be fingered and shaped.

This cave unfolds to my nudge, which
seems gentle but is hard as steel.

Coils of infinite steel are my secret.
Within this shadowless cave I am not confused
I think I am a fish, or a small seal.
I have an impulse to swim, but without
moving; *she* moves and I drift after. . . .
I am a trout silent and gilled, a tiny seal
a slippery monster knowing all secrets.
Where is she off to now?—in high heels.
I don't like the jiggle of high heels.
On the street we hear horns, drills, feel sleeves,
feel rushes of language moving by
and every stranger has possibly
my father's face.

Now we are in bed.
Her heart breathes quiet and I drink blood.
I am juicy and sweet and coiled.
Her dreams creep upon me through nightmare slots of
    windows
I cringe from them, unready.
I don't like such pictures.
Morning . . . and the safety of the day brings us
bedroom slippers, good.
Day at home, comfort in this sac,
three months from my birthday I dream
upon songs and eerie music, angels' flutes
that tear so stern upon earthly anger
(now they are arguing again).
Jokes and unjokes, married couple,
they clutch each other in water
I feel him nudge me but it is by accident.
The darkness of their sacs must be slimy with dead tides
and hide what they knew of ponds and knotty ropes of
    lilies.

It forsakes them now, cast into the same bed.
The tide throws them relentlessly into the same bed.
While he speaks to her I suck marrow from her bones.
It has a grainy white taste, a little salty.
Oxygen from her tremendous lungs taste white too
but airy bubbly, it makes me dizzy . . . !

She speaks to him and her words do not matter.
Marrow and oxygen matter eternally. They are mine.
Sometimes she walks on concrete, my vehicle,
sometimes on gravel, on grass, on the
blank worn tides of our floors at home.
She and he, months ago, decided not to kill me.
I rise and fall now like seaweed fleshed to fish, a surprise.
I am grateful.
I am waiting for my turn.

JOYCE CAROL OATES

The Recovery Room: Lying-in

Diapered in hospital linen,
my public seam stitched back into secrets,
I itch and heal in my crib, wrapped
in scopolamine. My lips like asbestos,
I can't make it
out of the medicine. Something has happened:
my belly has gone
flaccid, ersatz as sponge. Screwed
on this centripetal ache, I fix on pain

and breathe it like an element.
My neighbor-women are bad-mouthing the mothers-
in-law whose sons brought them to this.
We've been had. Joyful and dopey
we roll in our girlish paranoias.
The nurses want to sleep with the doctor; they wait
for my blood pressure to go down.
I try to climb, the walls shrug me off.
In my unique visiting hour I am visited
with guests witty beyond belief; before I can answer
the drug subsides, those pretend bastards are gone.

Back in my skull, out of love with the obstetrician,
I read my tag to prove I'm sensible.
The orderly wheels me upstairs to meet my daughter.

Funnyface, sweet heart,
this ordeal has almost nothing to do with love.

HELEN CHASIN

Waiting for the Doctor

I hear the doctor's loud success
booming to the anteroom,
my convent girl legs
criss-crossed at the ankles
narrowing the chapel where love huffs
like a wolf in the gray light
of redemptive sex.

Eucharistic body, tasty wafer,
Bristol-Cream sherry tapping through my veins,
Catholic outcome of a priest-father,
medieval mother on the guest bed of the parish,
witnessed by an ivory angel
and a watercolor Christ.

Waiting for the doctor, his loud success,
I think: my mother's breasts at thirty
tightening in my father's palms,
a crack inside her plaster flesh
widening for life,
my infant body's instant flush.

Disgusting girl—female scum, dirty secretions
attendant on woman's time, my mother thought
tying the parcel to mail me away.
I, reared on the assembly line,
factory for molding children into nuns.
Orphanage cookie, my cookie-self

waiting for the doctor
to come and view my masterworks:
assemblages of bone, mid-symphysial stage of decay,
sculptures for love programmed to fail,
but doubling cells under my flesh humming like a
    laundromat
a 9-lb. load to cart in and out of next year's bed.

COLETTE INEZ

Morning Song

Love set you going like a fat gold watch.
The midwife slapped your footsoles, and your bald cry
Took its place among the elements.

Our voices echo, magnifying your arrival. New statue.
In a drafty museum, your nakedness
Shadows our safety. We stand round blankly as walls.

I'm no more your mother
Than the cloud that distils a mirror to reflect its own slow
Effacement at the wind's hand.

All night your moth-breath
Flickers among the flat pink roses. I wake to listen:
A far sea moves in my ear.

One cry, and I stumble from bed, cow-heavy and floral
In my Victorian nightgown.
Your mouth opens clean as a cat's. The window square

Whitens and swallows its dull stars. And now you try
Your handful of notes;
The clear vowels rise like balloons.

SYLVIA PLATH

The Unwanted

Instead of you, I choose the blood.
Before your splash, that drag,
Rank stuff, but sure.
It is not fired through.
It is not dangerous like you.
Rationing lightning.

I cannot see the seed you are
Tipping my life
To madness or to worse.
Your growth kills mine.
So tinily you eat me all
To shreds.
I draw you out.
Godless, no mother
I have neither breath
Nor spirit to give up.

Mite, maggot, ovum, sperm,
What are you?
My neat trick, my sweet genesis.
Unbearable. Unborn.

MARY GORDON

102

The Abortion

Somebody who should have been born
is gone.

Just as the earth puckered its mouth,
each bud puffing out from its knot,
I changed my shoes, and then drove south.

Up past the Blue Mountains, where
Pennsylvania humps on endlessly,
wearing, like a crayoned cat, its green hair,

its roads sunken in like a gray washboard;
where, in truth, the ground cracks evilly,
a dark socket from which the coal has poured,

Somebody who should have been born
is gone.

the grass as bristly and stout as chives,
and me wondering when the ground would break,
and me wondering how anything fragile survives;

up in Pennsylvania, I met a little man,
not Rumpelstiltskin, at all, at all . . .
he took the fullness that love began.

Returning north, even the sky grew thin

like a high window looking nowhere.
The road was as flat as a sheet of tin.

Somebody who should have been born
is gone.

Yes, woman, such logic will lead
to loss without death. Or say what you meant,
you coward . . . this baby that I bleed.

ANNE SEXTON

The Empty Woman

The empty woman took toys!
　　In her sisters' homes
Were little girls and boys.

The empty woman had hats
To show. With feathers. Wore combs
In polished waves. Wooed cats

And pigeons. Shopped.
Shopped hard for nephew-toys,
Niece-toys. Made taffy. Popped

Popcorn and hated her sisters,
Featherless and waveless but able to
Mend measles, nag noses, blast blisters

And all day waste wordful girls
And war-boys, and all day
Say "Oh God!"—and tire among curls

And plump legs and proud muscle
And blackened school-bags, babushkas, torn socks,
And bouffants that bustle, and rustle.

GWENDOLYN BROOKS

Reflections on a Womb
Which Is Called "Vacant"

for SDB

1.
Charmed as a brown wicker nest
ready with blue paisley napkins,
just as empty as next summer's picnic basket
you are. You are
my timekeeper; my monthly wink;
my wrinkled sac full of bloody distance.

2.
My student helps me spend $15
on sports and hunting magazines:
the junior-high-problem-child-room decor.
He stays dull even when he looks
at photos of puffy eyed boxers and

rock calved runners, deerskins
and blood guttered knives.
I watch him and wonder
if his edges will come into focus.

3.

The princess took the thorn from his paw, splinted his
wing, chattered and sang him into a dark green sleep—
did all the things a woman does for an injured dragon.
But this princess did something else. When his paw
healed and he could flex his wing, she kissed him on the
forehead and walked him out the door.

It was that kissing and walking that made him rattle his
head and shut his eyes tight as filberts. While they were
shut, he searched himself. Nope (feeling here). Nope
(feeling there). So, he was not a prince in disguise.
He was a dragon dressed like a dragon. But healthy and
strong and kissed on the forehead dragons can do some-
    thing
else too.

When the princess turned to go back into her own warm
house, he caught her hand and led her to his place, his
burnt orange crack in the seawall. They sat on soft
    pillows
and he served tea and they listened to the waves ssush—
ssush against the sun-colored skin of that cave.

4.
The recurrent dream hold:
I am crouching in the corner
of a handball court. I know that I am
wearing a grey hospital gown and my eyes

are black as powder kegs, round as echoes.
I am crouching in the corner
because of the clicking yellow hands,
the bone whittled fingers which are poking
and digging and scratch-scratching
at my head full of ammunition.

     5.
Awake, I am beautiful.
I am loved with a peppermint affection.
When I open a window, sparkly air
fills the room. Curtains like eyelids flutter
with tiny secrets. This house I live in
has pockets of magic.

                    JEANINE HATHAWAY

The Children

Sometimes it seems
they came from nowhere,
arrived one Spring,
their quick minds perched on my fence
like precarious birds,
their limbs—wild iris
along my narrow road,

Having erased that time
when love pulled eagerly
at the thighs and the taking of seed

was a contrived joy,
and my belly, a ripe, golden sun.

It is as if
I never planned to bear them
turned suddenly to a gift
    of young voices.

Yes, they are here, and firm
eating my days—wind rascals,
ogres.

I love them,
wanting them gone.

Susan MacDonald

5

Sister, let the rain come down

For Anne, who doesn't know

Tonight you broke into my dreams
and I remembered yesterday when
your eyes retreated
before the people on the street
and you clutched my arm
hard. In the midst of our
talk and silences your
bitter secrets spilled
like fog over the buildings
of the ugly city where we walked.
The time passed so slowly. Finally
I said goodbye and they led
you away to the place where
you could pound the walls
and write your delicate poems.
Sister, let the rain come down:
there will never be
enough crying between us.

GAIL FOX

The Disconnection

Strings lay all about
She told me
Strings and threads lay all about
And none of them connected
Or touched her outstretched hand.
She held out her hand to me,
It seems a year behind
She held out her hand
And I reached back with mine.
But the strings and threads tied up her brain
And she cried in anguish
She cried my name
Let go my hand to cradle her head
And now she sits alone
She sits and cradles her head
Afraid that it will roll away,
Too tired to cut it off.

RITA MAE BROWN

A Dream of Women

I had
a dream of women, dark,
under water
so beautiful they hurt you
crossing a room
grocery carts piled high
with feminine graces, babies and poetry
their men blind with passion and greatly
envied

What literal seasons,
the days we want for our mind are
warmer—the fish swim,
the slot machines
chunk out solidly the thoughts
that are winners

This winter
women cry in their rooms alone
the streets come a glitter
photographs go dark on the walls
as though deep under water

What lack of mercy
have we given ourselves to.
Malignant armies of angels
inhabit the night

restlessly walking
the abandoned tracks calling
the flowers beauty
the empty shacks
home

Drifting

To live in
myself,

not thinking about.

Taking a canoe,
two girls,

down the river

with the blur of autumn
in the river water,

down large smears of red
that ran when we

paddled, the cluster
of willow

yellow where
the leaves fell.

In this slanty light

suspended, the canoe
stood still

on the water, the lovely

reflections not daring
to breathe,

the black surface of
water all dappled

with pollen. Though the dark
river ached
with its knowledge,

regrets; it
was not the day for them:

live on, live on.
We bent to the paddles.

KATHLEEN SPIVACK

The Sleeping Fury

You are here now,
Who were so loud and feared, in a symbol before me,
Alone and asleep, and I at last look long upon you.

Your hair fallen on your cheek, no longer in the
    semblance of serpents,
Lifted in the gale; your mouth, that shrieked so, silent.
You, my scourge, my sister, lie asleep, like a child,
Who, after rage, for an hour quiet, sleeps out its tears.

The days close to winter
Rough with strong sound. We hear the sea and the forest,
And the flames of your torches fly, lit by others,
Ripped by the wind, in the night. The black sheep for
    sacrifice
Huddle together. The milk is cold in the jars.

All to no purpose, as before, the knife whetted and
    plunged,
The shout raised, to match the clamor you have given
    them.
You alone turn away, not appeased; unaltered, avenger.

Hands full of scourges, wreathed with your flames and
    adders,
You alone turned away, but did not move from my side,
Under the broken light, when the soft nights took the
    torches.

At thin morning you showed, thick and wrong in that
   calm,
The ignoble dream and the mask, sly, with slits at the
   eyes,
Pretence and half-sorrow, beneath which a coward's
   hope trembled.

You uncovered at night, in the locked stillness of houses,
False love due the child's heart, the kissed-out lie, the
   embraces,
Made by the two who for peace tenderly turned to each
   other.

You who know what we love, but drive us to know it;
You with your whips and shrieks, bearer of truth and
   of solitude;
You who give, unlike men, to expiation your mercy.

Dropping the scourge when at last the scourged
   advances to meet it,
You, when the hunted turns, no longer remain the
   hunter
But stand silent and wait, at last returning his gaze.

Beautiful now as a child whose hair, wet with rage and
   tears
Clings to its face. And now I may look upon you,
Having once met your eyes. You lie in sleep and forget
   me.
Alone and strong in my peace, I look upon you in yours.

Louise Bogan

Sisters

Can I easily say,
I know you of course now,
no longer the fellow-victim,
reader of my diaries, heir
to my outgrown dresses,
ear for my poems and invectives?
Do I know you better
than that blue-eyed stranger
self-absorbed as myself
raptly knitting or sleeping
through a thirdclass winter journey?
Face to face all night
her dreams and whimpers
tangled with mine,
sleeping but not asleep
behind the engine drilling
into dark Germany,
her eyes, mouth, head
reconstructed by dawn
as we nodded farewell.
Her I should recognize
years later, anywhere.

ADRIENNE RICH

Patty, 1949-1961

Buried under a flat stone, but beside
  Some rich man's child, so that the wide
Wings of a limestone angel shield them both,
  My sister lies, who plighted troth
Early, as children in the old days did,
  With a sallow and unwanted
Suitor. "She is our own angel," I said,
  Thinking: Christ! What does being dead
Mean to a "vegetable," a tendril-haired pup
  That through moist eyes looked up
To people talking? Do her tortured limbs
  After convulsions enjoy their dim
Repose? I try to forget the puppetry
  I slept through, the reality
Of a scream in the night. Like Ishmael
  I floated on top of the Evil.
There are fancies: that by established right
  Of the first-born I am twice as bright
As I should be—my plumage, a plunder;
  That I can write only under
Her guidance—her sibyl spirit, my muse.
  Help me now! I wanted to lose
Myself that same June day your face turned black
  And I struggled to force breath back
Into your throat that was gummed shut with slime
  And could not. It was the last time
For a miracle. To teach me I ought

Not to want one, not yet, you brought
Me the arcanum in our poison kiss:
   Falling over the precipice,

Dying twice patience of Eurydice.
   (Go flower child, in peace bloom free.)

SHARON MAYER LIBERA

The Story of Good

for Barbara Green

Little robber girl, you sleep
on a blue pillow. The most difficult thing
in the world you will ever have to do
is get up each morning
and this you have done for me.
You have taken a third of my life from me
and sticky as a robber you come back
for more every day.

Why are you crying? Today is Wednesday,
turquoise, and green will follow, then purple.
Scarlet, we start again.
I will sing your lesson to you
and maybe you will hear a lesson,
or maybe just the sound, or tell me something
it reminds you of, from long before.

Yesterday we learned peasants and kings,
the rugs they hung, how cold their feet

must have been. Today is spoons:
a newborn litter of possum can be placed
in the bowl of a small spoon,
four baby hummingbirds can sit there
and this is what their small beaks point to:
among the stars in the sky, there is one
for Spelling, one for Numbers, one for Love.

Listen to the toys. You are more surprising
than what they said on Christmas morning
and you are prettier than the bear.
On your head there is real fur; your eyes
move in more directions.

All around you are kites. Why are we flying them?
We let them up and watch, or try to run with them.
The thin string in your hand is a wish,
and all that holds bright paper to the ground,
or lets it go.
What do you feel? Sad as Barbara,
it flies away from you, a rare bird.
Is there anyone who does not understand?

Seven bearded oranges have frightened you away.
You have put yourself in the wastebasket,
a bad grade.
I have turned sometimes, expecting someone larger,
but the fierce things you say are in a small body
and I cannot fit
down that tunnel anymore but only call and call
    and ask you
Barbara, what are you doing down there?

Listen, this is the day the dervishes turn,
each holding in his deep sleeve a magic bean
with twelve elephants inside
all telling the Story of Good:
come and play oh yes

PHYLLIS JANIK

If you saw a Negro lady

If you saw a Negro lady
sitting on a Tuesday
near the whirl-sludge doors of
Horn & Hardart on the main drag
of downtown Brooklyn

solitary and conspicuous as plain
and neat as walls impossible to
fresco and you watched her self-
conscious features shape about
a Horn & Hardart teaspoon
with a pucker from a cartoon

she would not understand
with spine as straight and solid
as her years of bending over floors
allowed

skin cleared of interest by a ruthless
soap   nails square and yellowclean
from metal files

sitting in a forty-year-old flush
of solitude and prickling
from the new white cotton blouse
concealing nothing she had ever noticed
even when she bathed and never
hummed a bathtub tune nor knew one

If you saw her square
above the dirty
mopped-on antiseptic floors
before the rag-wiped table tops

little finger   broad and stiff
in heavy emulation of a cockney

mannerism

would you turn her treat
into surprise observing
happy birthday

JUNE JORDAN

Coming Out

the first person I loved
was a woman   my passion
for her lasted thirty years

and was not returned
she never let me suck her nipples
she kept secrets between her legs
she told me men would love me
for myself   she couldn't tell me
ways to love myself
she didn't know

Mother, I would like to help you
swim back against the foaming river
to the source of our
incestuous fears
but you're so tired
out beyond the breakers
and I am upstream among my sisters
spawning

JACQUELINE LAPIDUS

Miniatures IV.
Mute the Hand Moves
from the Heart

Mute
the hand moves from the heart

upon the breast of her sleeping:
moves as if it reacht to pluck roses from a garden

but wore no quilted glove
braving all for love.

Now the lips are lightly open
like a robin's.

Now a whole choir is rising
of boys, above the sleeping head, in trees

giving psalm
and ease.

LYNN STRONGIN

sailing in crosslight

for Cathy

touch my hand as though it were an old coin
or the single drop of water
in a morning buttercup or the lines
you trace with your fingertips
on the face of the face beside yours
bind our days together
with a thin gold chain
like the one i find at the opening
in your shirt
you move about my thoughts
as in the room of a lover,
still asleep, disturbing the space
with your presence, drifting
toward her like smoke

ANITA SKEEN

125

Woman

I am caught up in her;
    A child at seaside play
    Lifted by the tidal wave.

I am possessed by her;
    Jesus' eyes in a painting
    Follow you.

She wraps me in her belly
    From
    Across the room.

JANE CHAMBERS

From: First Aspen

Written for a young woman painter, Alexandra

A sensuous Latin poet, now I will go off with a thermos
of coffee, and book of Virgil.
Laughing suddenly, strike a match but the flame's blown

out by desert wind.
Then I hold my head in my hands
with the ridiculous joy of the whole thing:

Young girl, you have made life
joyful again.
(From silence one comes—to it, returns.)

The aspens! each trembling branch
undone
by halo around the young leaves in the year's mature sun.

All artists
are aged
in compassion.

I am not so capable of Platonic love as it seems
especially now they are suddenly burning piñon
in New Mexico evenings.

Oh love that *sustains!*
for which I burn: Love that draws the tiredness from,
strong hands on a back, to sleep without pain.

So I turned mean?
said you were young:
It was the earthy gutsy mark of longing:

Salt, the sweat: THE TRUE MARK.
And she will not die whom I loved.   I'm unstrung:
It's dirty luck, that old bird.

But somenight I'll creep up in dark old raincoat
lay hands on you,
and wheeling round you'll suddenly know I seek you.

I'd pass thru dark train windows;
I'd press the monkish curls back from your cheek
molding a statue, instead of hacking poems out of love.

Van Gogh love!
young Russian! What are we to become who are
idealized *even in passion?*

I kiss lips paler than . . .
I touch a forehead in dream, thought springs from.
I hold hands—nervous and young.   First aspen.

This is where sorrow begins.

                         *

Apology. Hand shaping air;
holy smell of wood, the mathematical certainty
in your studio-kitchen:

balance of numbers,
beatitude of oil,
steady adding

steady breathing in marriage in your home.
As to mine?   feet moving thru memory.
Life is infinite subtraction:

Oh I can bite the orange rind
well as the next man.
But my palms shine.

I cannot wait till the aspens fall,
leave off being gold,
we may grind them underfoot like crushing out
   cigarettes.

Not cry
how we might have held
the cup more to our lips.

Sweetheart there is a brown wind here.
It will sink with the monotony of the passing year.
The words choke in my mouth

as if my hair were blown backward by that wind
which drove you to me,
which drove you to find me.

Neither by my poems nor your art will anyone ever be
quite able to explain our affair.
But it glows in sun (like the little hounds

released from hunt):
It is warm, it is here—
stretched out, relaxed by the fire.

You will rise at night
to brush back your monkish hair,
and perhaps tone down the color of the girl's cheek

in the picture. I may temper my poem, not so tender.
But today, I would have struck
the first aspen from earth to bring you, in its original
    flame:

Passion—Has it any other name?

*

Sapphic Love! Sculptress of far more than stone. Alex.
"I love everything about women. . . ."
I love to watch water receding from stone, after the storm

leaving the pure form:
Nervous, earthly woman, you are reaching now
to the marrow of my bone.

LYNN STRONGIN

Sayre

(Woman Professor)

The men in her department envied her.
She was too handsome, had published too many poems.
So, she'd tone down:

she wore olive-drab all that autumn
said she was in a dry season
could not write a single poem.

But her cheeks
took on the flush
of a woman riding.

Hand-to-hip she'd
breathe in the air
of evening.   The casual woman.

Sayre!
She'd claim she was a lonely woman
and besides had a bad spine.   Who'd envy her?

So intense that her fist
would smash glass
a Sunday evening.

But she'd flush a whole nest of quail
out of hiding
without so much as a shotgun   (or a sound.)

Camouflaged
broods of poems came.
The poem for her was—love's occasion.

She'd rise after, with that radiance
of a woman to meet her lover, eye shining
face to face.

Not one of the men guessed it was another woman.
So handsomely she moved, so darkly as through glass.

LYNN STRONGIN

instructions

for Pat Collins

let us not make apologies
nor give excuses
for the way things went
this last time around
does anyone ever get over
first love
we who wear our hearts upon our sleeves
must realize the danger of such exposure
the sun melts even the deepest snow

ducks who refuse to leave
their pond in winter
must remember hungry dogs
travel fast
they say that time heals all wounds
that a smile is the pathway
to a bright and happy life

i say bind your heart
with wire so it is not split
by a flower
hold it firm
so the wounds do not open
themselves
look how the land slips
from itself
and crumbling
erodes
endurance is possible
under the proper conditions
set your own

i am done with candles
and stained glass
have no time for puzzles
or naive promises
of the young
accept no more bones
though they come wrapped
in silver ribbon
be too smart
wear black gloves
to wring the days from your hands
and try to stifle

the voice inside proclaiming
"this is not it
this is not it"

ANITA SKEEN

Lesbian Poem

*dedicated to those who turned immediately
from the contents page to this poem*

After centuries of dissecting
Joan of Orleans
as deranged and sexually perverted
objective naturally historians of late
have taken to cleaning up her image.
The final indignity.

It seems, you see, there was a woman
named Haiviette,
with whom Joan lived, loved, slept,
and fought in battle,
whom scholars now say only was
"a girlhood friend"
splashing their filthy whitewash over
what must have been a bed
even Saint Catherine and Saint Brigid smiled upon.

In addition, it would appear
that Margaret Murray, a woman witchcraft scholar,

has found evidence that Joan was Wica, after all.
Did you know that The Maid is traditionally one
of the names that refers to the Coven's High Priestess?
See Murray's *The Witch-Cult in Western Europe*
for further guerrilla news.

Haiviette's name, at last, burns through their silence.
Joan's ashes flicker in our speech again.
Such bones as theirs
rattle with delight
wherever women love or lie together
on the night before
we go to war.

ROBIN MORGAN

tell our daughters

each is beautiful
a woman's life
makes it (that awareness)
through her touch

    descendants
of strict age
set against vanity

not secure in loveliness

a girl is born

like a little bird opening its wing
she lifts her face
in a down of feathers

a rose
    opens its leaves
with such a natural care
that we give words for
petal deep
in the imagination

                    a word becomes
                    a bitter thing
                    or a word is
                    an imagination

tell our daughters   they are
fragile as a bird
strong as the rose
deep as a word

and let them make
their own growing time

                    big with tenderness

                    BESMILR BRIGHAM

Saying Goodbye

I have watched you
on evenings while we met
together, shoes off
hair down, cross-legged
before the coffee tables,
the cheeses, pretzels, cakes;
coffee mugs, wine bottles:
planning, sympathizing, criticizing,
listening, complaining, celebrating,
yes, crying:
yes, toes knees elbows
curving into cups,
hair onto breasts,
a circle:

Pat,
your cheek bones shadowed
from pain and its aftermath,
your combat boots, delicate hips,
low voice keen mind worrying
Alexa's baby life suddenly twining
round your own
working always, thinking
your thin fingers

Zoya,
white hair pulled into a pony tail

full breasts, you recall
their youthful splendor
off to London alone
three sons, husband left at home
sure, unsure
your wise good sense and laughter
and when you speak of your cello
it is there, perceptive, resonant,
there as with sureness
your bow moves across
the girl inside your matron air
is sure, unsure
with a shy beauty still

Maurean,
you quietly remember for us
yourself as nun in coif and mantle,
all that red flame hair
shut away beneath the black habit,
but quietly you left
now you nurse your baby
your hair gleaming in the lamplight
your striped jeans, two babies, new PhD,
pale freckled skin tired eyes
new rituals

De Ann,
sloping waist
dark hair long against round breasts
pale beauty fighting out of silence
the asking to be protected
fighting hard against soft voice
soft skin girl bride wife child
knowing you will not break

Bonnie,
fringe of hair
round glasses round eyes white socks
gallant Bonnie laughing at yourself
your terror when a cat comes in
the love you pour over child Amanda
I see you driving those miles
to State College, clutching the huge wheel,
peering into the rain
studying into endless nights
as if your heart would break

Maura,
you're not so tough
your peasant blouses
sturdy legs, sandals, grin
your hands always working
at some task or craft
deft needle pen string
while you ponder, suggest
you stand firm as you question
and work things
out

Pat,
silent critic,
not lightly do you pass judgement
upon me, upon life
you hoe your own road
alone, among us all
with smudges beneath your eyes
your face bent over a cigarette
your beautiful legs, your cool;
nervous fingers, sophisticated drawl

shirt unbuttoned low at the neck
with me and yet distant always
rarely do you relax
intelligent, committed
to the causes of all
unjustly sentenced to life
I respect your judgements
yet wish that you would not
always have to

Amy,
I put you in this poem
without any distance at all
with your cleverness, your humor
the girlish lightness
that is nearly gone now
from having been hurt without much reason
except that you were getting too smart
straight long hair losing its blondness
bright rimmed glasses over gay eyes
sensuous breasts in an old jersey
wearing your brother's jeans, tall
laughing
our heads together
in endless conversations
revelations consolations
the more that we knew of each other
the more we liked it

Now me,
the ninth,
what do you think of me?
I've pushed myself upon you all
I've tried to hold back

and generally couldn't
I've given you
everything I could get hold of
to give
I am fierce and emotional
too frightened too proud
what have I given you?

Now I am breaking the circle
which will close again
without me, close over me
I will go away
leaving behind the circle
leaving you behind
in the lamplight, talking:
talking of what has happened
of what to do
planning revolution
or salvation
without me.

SUZANNE JUHASZ

My People

When I was a child
my family was my people.
I was not proud of us
but thought we were unique,
and knew our family history

by heart, even songs
from my grandfather's growing up.

When I was an adolescent
I thought the Jews were my people.
I never said it that way,
but everyone I knew was Jewish
and the deep sorrow of Jewish prayers
made me proud of my suffering:
oh God (oh Boyfriend)
why hast thou forsaken me?

As a young married woman
my husband was my people
in a nation of two
with bedroom sized boundaries.
We shared some sacred truths
and our own language
everyone else was on the outside.

Now I say that women are my people.
I call us mirror-sisters
because when I look inside your words
I see myself.
I call us Awakening Nation
because I think of us as a baby
discovering its body
and the power of its cry.
I call us a people
although we have just begun to move together.
What unites us is not our past
but our future.

MARGERY HIMEL

141

6

Does the patient die if nobody knows

Truth

Does the typewriter type
If nobody hears it?

Nobody hears it.
There are no letters
There are no mailmen
There is no mail

The white blizzard subsides.

Does the patient die
If nobody knows?

Nobody knows.
He does not die.
Reels of film
Run backwards,
Wheels of a watch.

There are no funerals
There are no graves
There is no death.
Relatives are dandelions on stalks.

Yesterday, a tree was seen walking
By a dark man
Its thin brown feet
Covering the earth like a net

Its branches grew up, up
Holding the sun
Sweet orange
Caught in its net.

Tree leaves clatter masses
For leaves.

SUSAN FROMBERG SCHAEFFER

Housewife

What can be wrong
That some days I hug this house
About me like a shawl, and feel
Each window like a tatter in its skin,
Or worse, bright eyes I must not look through?

Now my husband stands above me
As high as ever my father did
And I am in that house of dolls, which,
When young I could not shrink to.

I feel the shrinkage in each bone.
No matter what I do, my two girls
Spoil like fruit. Already they push us back
Like too-full plates. They play with us
Like dolls.

The road before the house is like a wish
That stretches out and out and will not

Stop, and the smallest hills are built
Like steps to the slippery moon,
But I
Circle this lit house like any moth
And see each day open its fingers
To disclose the stone—which hand?
Which hand? and the stone in both.

Once, I drove my car into a tree.
The bottles in the back
Burst like bombs, tubular glass beasts,
Giving up the ghost. My husband
Thought it was the road. It was.
In the rear-view mirror, it curved and curled,
Longer and stronger than the road ahead,
A question of perspective, I thought then.
I watched it til it turned, and I did not.
I breathed in pain like air,
As if, I, the rib, had cracked.

I did not feel this pain, not then,
Almost in my mouth. I wiggle this life
And find it loose. Like my girls,
I would pull it out, would watch
Something new and white
Push like mushrooms from the rich red soil.
But there is just this hole, this bone.

So I live inside my wedding ring,
Inside its arch,
Multiplying the tables of my days,
Rehearsing the lessons of this dish, that sleeve,
Wanting the book that no one wrote,
Loving my husband, my children, my house

With this pain in my jaw,
Wanting to go.

Do others feel like this? Where do they go?

Her Story

They gave me the wrong name, in the first place.
They named me Grace and waited for a light and agile
   dancer.
But some trick of the genes mixed me up
And instead I turned out big and black and burly.

In the second place, I fashioned the wrong dreams.
I wanted to dress like Juliet and act
Before applauding audiences on Broadway.
I learned more about Shakespeare than he knew about
   himself.
But of course, all that was impossible.
"Talent, yes," they would tell me,
"But an actress has to look the part."
So I ended up waiting on tables in Harlem
And hearing uncouth men yell at me:
"Hey, momma, you can cancel that hamburger
And come on up to 102."

In the third place, I tried the wrong solution.
The stuff I drank made me deathly sick

And someone called a doctor.
Next time I'll try a gun.

NAOMI LONG MADGETT

A Work of Artifice

The bonzai tree
in the attractive pot
could have grown eight feet tall
on the side of a mountain
till split by lightening.
But a gardener
carefully pruned it.
It is nine inches high.
Everyday as he
whittles back the branches
the gardener croons
it is your nature
to be small and cosy,
domestic and weak
how lucky, little tree,
to have a pot to grow in.
With living creatures
one must begin very early
to dwarf their growth:
the bound feet,
the crippled brain,
the hair in curlers,

the hands you
love to touch.

MARGE PIERCY

The Rebel

When I
die
I'm sure
I will have a
Big Funeral

Curiosity
seekers

coming to see
if I
am really
Dead

or just
trying to make
Trouble

MARI E. EVANS

Interview with a Tourist

You speed by with your camera and your spear
and stop and ask me for directions

I answer there are none

You ask me why the light here
is always the same colour;
I talk about the diffuse
surfaces, angles of refraction

You want to know why there are
no pleasant views, no distances,
why everything crowds close to the skin

I mention the heavier density
here, the thickness, the obsolescence of vistas

You ask me why the men are starved and silver
and have goggle eyes
and why the women are cold tentacled flowers

I reply with a speech about Nature

You ask me why I can't love you

It is because you have air in your lungs
and I am an average citizen

Once, when there was history
some obliterating fact occurred,
no solution was found

Now this country is underwater;
we can love only the drowned

MARGARET ATWOOD

Evaporation Poems

1.
I would like to be as mobile as my mind
I had a religious aunt who was
And of course, she died
(She flew out a window into the Ideal)

So much noise, the water in stems,
The workings of animal teeth
And intestines;
Such foolishness, she decided,
You have to disconnect the pain
From the sense of loss,
Until all you feel is nostalgia and boredom,
Until you're free from distraction

The trouble begins when no one wants anything in par-
    ticular,
And you have to decide what to give them in return;
"It's like deciding anything," she said,
"Even transformation has its price"

2.

The dead complain of having inadequate information
They've been playing with matches and razor blades for
  some time now, and nothing has been revealed.
They're too aesthetic to pay much attention to detail;
Somehow, though, they've managed to obtain college
  degrees
And roses spring up in their hair
At the mention of death, or dying

They sense that something perpetual, banal,
And quite routine is going on in the universe
They say it will make them crazy if they don't watch out

They're on the lookout for the future, and its
  "complications"
If you say that even the water's need is a simple one, they
  get upset

3.

All summer I have watched the water
Take whatever shape it can,
Whispering, "there is the past,
And the future, and between the two of them
You must be careful not to disappear"

Now I see so clearly on the days when rain turns to snow;
The wind passes along the surfaces of things,
The chill settles in around the place where I have moved
  with everything

KATHLEEN NORRIS

From 2nd Chance Man:
The Cigarette Poem

i sit clumsy in my flesh, my legs
stiff, thick.   i am
gemstones, collapsed and dried,
the magic bean nobody
wanted.   i am the size of
grief.   i am quiet and left
to sit with cats and
stoves and dripping faucets.
my socks dry on the bathroom rack.
the heat clicks on.   it is pale in here
and nothing moves.
the silence of photographs.
the silence of snow.   no one comes here except
by telephone.

i have been blind, blind.   drunk
on my own flesh.
circumstance and habit were the cloth mended to me
by hands i didnt even see, hands
buried in the wallpaper
of houses i only visited
in dreams.

ghost.   the hearse at the window.
raindrops, large as coffins, crawl

out of my legs toward the open space
of sidewalk.   out the window.
toward the next century.
ghost.
the hallway dark as a fish eye or
the evil eye.
dark.

it begins.   the family coming loose as little pictures.
it begins.   and they watch me.   and they are mostly
   dead.
and i
look back into them as though they were tunnels.
i fall asleep, rock
backward into a time i can not remember.
dreams break open and the earth
jumps loose.   i wake to things falling.
the dark is marked by stars, by dead places in the sky.

the beginning.   the road through graves that bead
like sweat on the skin.
the fire, the sacrificial lovemaking.   the path.
the language of cum awakening the spirit.
the spirit the song at the window,
the shape i crack open, make soft,
add to myself, my body thick
as honey.   i nurture the hole i was, fill it up.

FAYE KICKNOSWAY

The Man in the Dream Is Death

It appears to be the pampas
though grey at the edges
as if I am about to faint
and when I find the usual baby
this time about to be eaten
by a badger
I say the indians have done it
but when three men pass by
and one shows his face
I know who it is
though he later pretends
to be a rancher
his black wet-suit gives him away
and mine is the cutting horse
that tries to run him down
crashing down hills
finally stalled
at the cattle guard
despite the child I must balance
and a horse that will not
obey.

LYNNE BUTLER

Birthday Card for a Psychiatrist

Your friends come fondly to your living room
believing, my dear, that the occasion's mild.
Who still feels forty as a moral *crise*
in this, the Century of the Common Child?

Uncommon gifts, brought to mid-life in pain,
are not a prize. The age demands a cure
for tragedy and gives us brand-new charts
for taking down our psychic temperature.

Othello, of course, regrets having been aggressive,
Hamlet feels pretty silly to think he trusted
terms such as "art" and "honor" instead of "projection,"
and out on the moor King Lear feels maladjusted.

An arrogant richness of the human stuff
is not a value. Nobody wants to be
left holding the bag of himself when all the others
are a democratic homogeneity.

Prospero strips down to his underpants
to teach Miranda that fathers can be informal,
while Cleopatra, Juliet, Rosalind, Kate
fight for the golden apple labelled NORMAL.

In such a state, what laurels can poems bring,
what consolation, what wishes, what advice?

May your conflicts thin out with your hair? BE HAPPY?
We hope you're feeling well? We think you're nice?

Till Burnam Wood shall come to Dunsinane,
till time shall tell us what we really are,
till Responsibility, not Health, defines
the terms of living on this serious star,

to receive the trauma of birth and pass it on
is all we're here for. Yet we hope you realize
we're glad that forty years ago you came
to join us in this neurotic enterprise.

MONA VAN DUYN

The First Test

What is there they will not do to you?
They have their needles,
Their hammers, their knives.

They say, there is no symmetry,
We must chip, must chip.
They say, the wood grain is good
See that network of veins,

We must plane, must plane.
The cry
Is a dead bird
Stuck in your throat

Its tongue, tan tube
Ties around your vein,
Tight.

What is it, then?
There is no one to refuse
No voice that grows its own wall
Like a stone   saying *no*

They are opening the windows
The patients are flying out of the windows
Like bees

The city is covered with pollen
The puff-dusting sun.
The same eye
Sees the clock
The hand wound

Still ticking
Time contracts
An eye in the light
The same eye sees the dial
The noon mark is a line of flies

Six is a snake, rigid and pale
The eye averts to the sun,
It christens and blinds.

SUSAN FROMBERG SCHAEFFER

Womb Song

This is the most ridiculous womb!
It is a kind of hotel
And there are guests all over.
They keep arriving with square cardboard boxes
Of bakery cake, tied in red and white string.

In a corner, my fat aunt and my mother
Are discussing whether to license
My marriage to a *gentile*, a *goy*.
My grandfather keeps shouting
Cut her out! Cut her out!
(He means his will.)

My grandmother rocks in her corner
Like one of the fates.
She complains to anyone who will listen
About her bad eyes.
Her lenses are thicker than clam shells.

Meanwhile, I am trying to call you.
I am dragging the phone cord from closet to closet
But each door that I open
Turns into a room flooded with light.
It is like being inside a bulb.

People are hanging from the hangers in racks.
Privacy is impossible.

Each time that I reach you,
You say hello and hang up.
No one seems to notice the small animal

Or person who has come in
Through the sheet of plate glass.
The operator says she cannot
Possibly connect me when I am hanging
Here by my knees like a monkey
From the P.S. 206 jungle jim.

What a place!
I want to get out, or to let others in.
I am wrapping the black cord
Around my neck, noose of absences,
Noose of presences, presences.

Somewhere there is the scrape of a trunk
And a voice saying, not *that* case,
Take this.

SUSAN FROMBERG SCHAEFFER

The Invisible Woman

The invisible woman in the asylum corridor
sees others quite clearly,
including the doctor who patiently tells her
she isn't invisible—
and pities the doctor, who must be mad

161

to stand there in the asylum corridor
talking and gesturing to nothing at all.

The invisible woman has great compassion.
So, after a while, she pulls on her body
like a rumpled glove, and switches on her voice
to comfort the elated doctor with words.
Better to suffer this prominence
than for the poor young doctor to learn
he himself is insane.
Only the strong can know that.

ROBIN MORGAN

Evening in the Sanitarium

The free evening fades, outside the windows fastened
    with decorative iron grilles.
The lamps are lighted; the shades drawn; the nurses are
    watching a little.
It is the hour of the complicated knitting on the safe bone
    needles; of the games of anagrams and bridge;
The deadly game of chess; the book held up like a mask.

The period of the wildest weeping, the fiercest delusion,
    is over.
The women rest their tired half-healed hearts; they are
    almost well.
Some of them will stay almost well always: the blunt-
    faced woman whose thinking dissolved

Under academic discipline; the manic-depressive girl
Now leveling off; one paranoiac afflicted with jealousy.
Another with persecution. Some alleviation has been
  possible.

O fortunate bride, who never again will become elated
  after childbirth!
O lucky older wife, who has been cured of feeling
  unwanted!
To the suburban railway station you will return, return,
To meet forever Jim home on the 5:35.
You will be again as normal and selfish and heartless as
  anybody else.

There is life left: the piano says it with its octave smile.
The soft carpets pad the thump and splinter of the
  suicide to be.
Everything will be splendid: the grandmother will not
  drink habitually.
The fruit salad will bloom on the plate like a bouquet
And the garden produce the blue-ribbon aquilegia.
The cats will be glad; the fathers feel justified; the
  mothers relieved.
The sons and husbands will no longer need to pay the
  bills.
Childhoods will be put away, the obscene nightmare
  abated.

At the ends of the corridors the baths are running.
Mrs. C. again feels the shadow of the obsessive idea.
Miss R. looks at the mantel-piece, which must mean
  something.

LOUISE BOGAN

163

Her Application to Elysium

It consisted of 8 to 10 pages of short essays,
Much like the applications to colleges such as Ben-
    nington, or Sarah Lawrence
She wrote that she had always kept a certain distance
    from her surroundings;
This was in response to the first question, requesting
    name, address, and schools previously attended
The enclosed booklist revealed that she had read too
    many French pornographic novels,
And she confessed that she generally did what she was
    told.
    (This was confirmed by an ex-science teacher who
    wrote:
    "all she requires is a good slap across the backside,
    and she will move slowly in the desired direction")

When asked about her most meaningful relationships,
She prepared a list, carefully catalogued,
With cross-references:
The female peer, the male peer, the female teacher,
The male teacher, foreign nationals, vibrators of various
    shapes and sizes,
A policeman's horse she had befriended in Central Park,
A museum curator, her local Democractic assemblyman.
She was careful to explain what each symbolized,
    in the long run,
What each experience had done for her

To finish up,
She mentioned several virtues which she felt would par-
  ticularly recommend her to the desired kingdom;
A basic discomfort with things as they are,
The ability to live vicariously,
A limitless capacity for self-pity

She had a friend mail it for her;
And months later, she eagerly opened the little kit, which
    contained some embalming fluid, and a copy of the
    memoirs of Anais Nin,
And her eyes would not stop shining

KATHLEEN NORRIS

A Letter from a Friend

Sometimes this quiet settles in like a stone
in my stomach, all the weight

shifts down.   I feel so little.   Ask myself
what I feel, and it is the stone

settling downward.   My voice comes up
from a deeper space but speaks seldom.

I see the defined crease of the drapes
with their chinese farmers

and chinese junk and chinese river.   Or exactly
how the sun floods the white house

behind us.
I receive a letter from a friend who asks

can beauty approach technology?
I can only stare dumbly at it

and affirm everything.   The stone
is my father, my mother,

together we affirm even the woman
next door who likes vicious gossip

moving the transparent folds of her
curtains. . . .

the stone is the absence of habitual pain.
The stone is the light and the shadow

deepening within me, collecting
its moisture in a pool fit

for drinking.   Animals emerge, the presence
of new life unconcerned and later entirely

forgotten.   Anne, another friend, wrote
of the banyon tree in Jules Verne park.

Anne, you must swallow that tree.
A tree of great and valuable weight

going down easily as a seed.
You will become what you wanted,

the true nun of your sex and voice.

166

At night the birds and insects will hide

in you.

In the Hospital of the Holy Physician

In the hospital of the holy physician, I hear
no voices in the waiting room.
No nurses with needles take my name
or jab the beat of my harlequin fear,
    my jewel-in-the-heart
    that tried so long
    to make my life an art.

In the hospital of the holy physician I come
wearing the shape of sin
like a love-child under my skin.
The voices clotting my blood go numb.
    I do not sleep, I see
    rooms break like bones
    to set me free.

In the hospital of the holy physician, I move
toward the scalpel judiciously hurled
at my brain till healing has pearled
a pilgrimage on each rotten groove,
    shining and clear.
    In the pulse of my ruin
    I make my cure.

NANCY WILLARD

7

Now you are my literary ghost

A valley where I don't belong

The first cocks begin clearing the throat of morning—
Who's that walking up on Pettijean mountain?—
rasping their brass cries from outflung necks
as they dig their spurs in the clammy cellar air.
Windows upon the mountain trap the first light.
Their bronze and copper plumage is emerging
from the pool of dusk. Lustily they drill the ear
with a falsetto clangor strident as mustard
raising alarm   I   I   I live   I live!

I stand with a damp wind licking my face
outside this shabby motel where a man snores
who is tiring of me so fast my throat parches
and I twist the hem of my coat thinking of it.

"The rooster, or cock, is a symbol of male sexuality,"
the instructor said, elucidating Herrick.
You stuck me with spiky elbow and matchspurt glance.
We were eighteen: we both were dancers in the woods,
you a white doe leaping with your Brooklyn satyr.
Bones and sap, I rode in the mothering earth
tasting the tough grass and my dear's salty mouth,
open and swept, in a gale of dark feathers.

We owned the poems they taught us, Leda and Europa.
We struck the earth with our heels and it pivoted,
sacred wood of blossoming crab and hanging snake,
wet smoke close to the grass and a rearing sun.

That fruit has fallen. You were burned like a Greek
just before the last solstice, but without games.
I was not there. For a long while I hadn't been.

Now you are my literary ghost.
I with broken suitcase and plump hips, about
to be expelled from this man to whom I'm bound
by the moist cord of want and the skeins of habit,
a hitchhiker in the hinterland of Ozarks.

You hardened to an edge that slashed yourself
while I have eased into flesh and accommodation.
The cry of the mouse shrill and covetous in my fingers.
I cannot keep my hands from anything.
My curiosity has been a long disaster.
I fear myself as once I feared my mother.
Still I know no more inexorable fact
than that thin red leap of bone: I live, I live.
I and my worn symbols see up the sun.

MARGE PIERCY

Invocation to Sappho

Sappho
            Sister/Mother
                                    free-
souled, fire-hearted
Psappha of Mitylene on
sea-lapped Lesbos

miracle of a woman
                    (Strabo wrote)
now   now
            let me declare
devotion.

Not light years   love years
on how many love years
across fields of the dead
does your fragrance
travel to me?

Since maidenhood   in brain   blood
by you haunted
in my own armpits I have breathed
sweat of your passion
in the burning crotch of the lover
tasted your honey
heard   felt in my pulse
                        day-long
                                    night-through
lure of your song's beat
insistently echo.

By dust of five-and-twenty centuries
                            not smothered
by book-consuming flames of
the hate-filled churchmen
                        unsilenced
your fame only haloed   made
more splendid.

Sappho, little and dark,

the Beautiful, Plato called you
(though his Republic had
grudging use for poets)
Sappho, whose veins ran fire
                        whose nerves
quivered to loves illicit now
                        in your day
honored by the noblest
Sappho, all roses,
do we not touch
across the censorious years?

ELSA GIDLOW

Mythics

To RSF

1. ONDINE
All the cautionary tales of strange girls
could not prevent coming to this:
sea-changed, I dance in shallows
dripping feathery anklets
and splash in the tide (foamy,
opalescent) weedy hair eddying
in its elemental pull,
the fish princess who asked for legs
and bled into her footprints,
her scaly heart flaking until dawn.

2. CINDERELLA

In this domicile of cosmetic disasters
(dowager's hump, psoriasis, spinster's
breath, dropped arches) I queen it
over the slag heap, over the resident
hags. None of theirs! Changeling
beauty, domestic burden: I sift coal
like black diamonds—alien, determined
to make it out of this dreary household.

3. RAPUNZEL

Removed by that crone
I range in my cloister, closeted with
dreams of release, growing my hair
like foliage, gathering moss.
Ugly, covetous, my keeper rages at her ward,
her golden girl. Our bramble thickets lock
into a wall and darken my chamber.
You might find me
and I unbraid to your call,
glory in the fall of my crowning glory,
drop into living with my blind, punished hero.

4. RUMPELSTILTSKIN

I took instruction in love's ravel,
fabricated a homespun treasure
and dazzled my greedy regent into husbandry.
After the baby, complications set in.
Pursued by my useful, anonymous menace
and spinning frantic names, I twisted
in our blood bargain until a minister
told his funny story: how
the little man wove his grotesque forest circle,
the gleeful warp of my answer.

And when, dancing into a tantrum
he dropped out of the riddle
I kept my king, gold, child, and secret.

5. SNOW WHITE
Fled from the battle, hid
from the wicked queen's fatal plot,
I lie low and make do
with beauty and virtue
and cohabit with small men: friendly,
inadequate. This house,
my woodsy retreat, is easy
to keep in order. What could be more
innocent, except to dream,
latent and clothed, under glass
until the prince and his retinue
jar my crib and I am aroused,
passive, saved?

6. PSYCHE
In these nights, transported, I know
love's perfection: words like the heart's choke,
body's language, framed like a dream,
the ultimate dark secret.
Women have risked burning
for hours less extraordinary than these.
Love, waiting for your visit
I long for the dailiness, human rubs, usual
trials and flawed pleasures
this perpetual ecstasy denies.

7. BEAUTY (AND THE BEAST)
Whether it was the maxims about good hearts
and the limited value of pure esthetics

or something closer to danger—
once I saw him, the princelings and precepts went
neutral as oatmeal. He was ugly as sin:
animal heavings, flaccid mouth, agonized baboon stare,
pitted skin, hairshirted like a mistaken birth.
My cry mimicked pity.
Ladies, all's fair in
ignorance; I was young and easily moved.
Now, rewarded, I submit to his transfiguration.

HELEN CHASIN

A Conversation

For Isak Dinesen

As we stood on the crushed stone
Of the drive, it was as if
A spring landscape unrolled
Between. Colors deep
As gems—the tapestry,
Intricate and rich,
Of a lifetime. I was
Assumed into this world;
These emblematic hues
Shone like vintage wine:
Jet—that contains darkness
For those who have known the worst;
Beige—parchment-colored,
On which a burning glass

Etches the mind's runes;
Turquoise—that mood of green
And blue, field and sky—
Blending, to stand out.
Artist and woman moved there
Each in her separate light,
Clear-cut against a silver
Background of dream—all
Colors blend in silver,
A molten gong—whose full
Resonance an artist
Brocades upon the soul.

BARBARA HOWES

Aristophanes' Symposium

I have known it from the beginning
As though by fate
Disbelieving fate.
That we as one
Were divided by some awful hand
And I have searched the centuries for your face,
Hearing eons echo your name,
A muffled refrain drenched in longing.
Long have I yearned,
Spurning women
All women save the one I knew
In thick clouds of prehistory.
Even Helen was a bone

I threw to Paris
Outraged at her imperfection.
I toiled, a plaything of Cronos
From Genesis through silly flocks of years
Herding decades into the penumbra of my brain
Poking shadows of bleating days for your face.
The years slipped by
And I alone felt them go
No longer counting sheep
Too tired for counting sheep
But I will know you as you know me
And one day you will call me, "Woman."

RITA MAE BROWN

Diptych

(Based on events recorded in the Book of Esther. Had
it not been for Queen Vashti's refusing to obey the
king's command, there would have been no Queen
Esther.)

PART 1. QUEEN VASHTI: FIRST FEMINIST
You say the king commands that I appear
Before the seven princes and his friends?—
He must have made too merry with the wine!
I am the queen, not some slave dancing-girl
To entertain his guests, displaying charms
Reserved for royal eyes alone. Go back
And tell the king I, too, have many guests
I would not leave. The wives of other men

Will honor my decision that a wife
Must have respect above a concubine.
Ahasuerus may divorce me—still
Our union's weak if this can come between:
Even a king may not command a queen!

PART 2. KING AHASUERUS: ROYAL MALE VIEWPOINT
Vashti had beauty like a perfect flower
Or some rare jewel, and a man has pride
To own perfection. I had shown my guests
(The seven princes) all that I possessed
In my vast kingdom, then gave them a feast
With friends within the palace. But I longed
To have them see my queen, my fairest treasure.
And so I sent for her. She was with guests,
Feasting the women—but that was no excuse
For not obeying me. In anger, then
I asked the wise men and the princes there
What should be done, and all agreed with me;
She set a bad example. Other wives
Hearing, might flout their husbands. So we drew
A law for all the Persians and the Medes,
Divorcing her, and spread the word abroad
So wives would honor husbands and obey.
Small punishment for such a public thing:
Even a queen must not defy a king.

VELMA WEST SYKES

Mercedes, Her Aloneness

1.
Her stiffening captor lies in wait
under the fronds of the palmetto.
Hamhock hands
arc to her breasts,
rennet mounds beneath a shift
of tapioca flowers.

2.
Give in, the heron creaks,
wing span greater than hands.
Go under,
below your heart the billowed waves.

3.
She goes. Mercedes bending wide-honed thighs
under the rawness of his hide.
Swimming the dusk with clogged ears,
salt in her nostrils.
Day's junk plumbing oblivious seas.

They spread the rhythm of their instant
over grit, stammering neon, veins
of asphalt hardening lawns
of balconied motels.

4.
Home. Sperm lashing her womb.

Lips pressed to the moon's
pole of wash on the shingled wall.

Doorslam's jolt. Muslin bind of sleep.
Crumpling flesh
dents the hour
with weights of breath.

    5.
The air crawling on all fours
secreting its slime into her pores,
in the singular print of her palm,
anointing aloneness.

COLETTE INEZ

for our lady

     yeh.
         billie.   if someone
had loved u like u
shud have been loved
ain't no tellen what
kinds of songs
           u wud have swung
gainst this country's wite mind.
or what kinds of lyrics
           wud have pushed us from
our blue / nites.
         yeh.   billie.

            if some blk / man
                              had reallee
            made u feel
                              permanentlee warm.
            ain't no tellen
                        where the jazz of yo/songs
                              wud have led us.

                                    SONIA SANCHEZ

Closer First to Earth

for Sylvia Plath

Complicity killed you. I know. I know
the man who black-balled your grant.
He is the forever paternalistic bastard
who knows best what is good for us.

I know the abyss, artist and woman
trying to reach each other across it,
that you couldn't quite build a bridge over,
not even a swaying, fragile reed one.

I would like to think I survived
by cleverness rather than by terror
of letting the wrong people have control.
I dared not let them rape my mind, too.

Wherever you are, high-wire artist,

I think, just possibly, instruction
from a woman juggler, closer first
to earth, might have saved your life.

ANNE HAZLEWOOD-BRADY

In Sylvia Plath Country

for Grace

The skin of the sea
has nothing to tell me.

I see her diving down
into herself—

past the bell-shaped jellyfish
who toll for no one—

& meaning to come back.

                    *

In London, in the damp
of a London morning,
I see her sitting,
folding & unfolding herself,
while the blood
hammers like rain
on her heart's windows.

This is her own country—
the sea, the rain
& death half rhyming
with her father's name.

Obscene monosyllable,
it lingers for a while
on the roof
of the mouth's house.

I stand here
savoring the sound,
like salt.

*

They thought your death
was your last poem:
a black book
with gold-tooled cover
& pages the color of ash.

But I thought different,
knowing how madness
doesn't believe
in metaphor.

When you began to feel
the drift of continents
beneath your feet,
the sea's suck,
& each
atom of the poisoned air,
you lost
the luxury of simile.

Gull calls, broken shells,
the quarried coast.
This is where America ends,
dropping off
to the depths.

Death comes
differently in California.
Marilyn stalled
in celluloid,
the frame stuck,
& the light
burning through.

Bronze to her platinum,
Ondine, Ariel,
finally no one

what could we tell you
after you dove down into yourself
& were swallowed
by your poems?

ERICA JONG

after reading sylvia plath:

i opened my door to this nutty witch.   i've been suicidal
all day after our conversation: serves me right for
   trying

to relate to a suicidal poet. her long fingers are not caught
in the grave: her cry lives in our mouths, i am not the only
person writing this & i am getting progressively more fright-
ened. the following poems came to me last week. they all
speak for both of us, i feel. none of them were deliber-
ately
like hers. the resemblance is uncanny.

    1.

ivy ivy trailing down your little suckers clutch the house
green life from my flesh, you call me sustenance;
(this aweful lonliness attracts people.)
they crowd around, "o, don't be lonely. i love you!"
i shrink back in fear (i've heard that line before)
i see their teeth. "just people"
i reassure myself, but cannot bear their clasp:
i believe you i believe you!
i cry, bursting free. . . .

ALTA

Wanting to Die

Since you ask, most days I cannot remember.
I walk in my clothing, unmarked by that voyage.
Then the almost unnameable lust returns.

Even then I have nothing against life.
I know well the grass blades you mention,
the furniture you have placed under the sun.

But suicides have a special language.
Like carpenters they want to know *which tools*.
They never ask *why build*.

Twice I have so simply declared myself,
have possessed the enemy, eaten the enemy,
have taken on his craft, his magic.

In this way, heavy and thoughtful,
warmer than oil or water,
I have rested, drooling at the mouth-hole.

I did not think of my body at needle point.
Even the cornea and the leftover urine were gone.
Suicides have already betrayed the body.

Still-born, they don't always die,
but dazzled, they can't forget a drug so sweet
that even children would look on and smile.

To thrust all that life under your tongue!—
that, all by itself, becomes a passion.
Death's a sad bone; bruised, you'd say,

and yet she waits for me, year after year,
to so delicately undo an old wound,
to empty my breath from its bad prison.

Balanced there, suicides sometimes meet,
raging at the fruit, a pumped-up moon,

leaving the bread they mistook for a kiss,

leaving the page of the book carelessly open,
something unsaid, the phone off the hook
and the love, whatever it was, an infection.

ANNE SEXTON

Flannery O'Connor

In this world
it is always Hallowe'en:
Masquers, faces askew, as if somebody stepped on the
    clay
before it was set.

Gargoyle perched on a city church
grinning at the jostling
bodies below:
They share a secret.

The angel slays
in the name of righteousness.

Love is forgotten,
buried under a pile of trashy magazines
in the corner,
naked thighs
and ragged lace.

Everything is mingy,
smelling of stale peach pits
as if the garbage had not
been carried out in a long time.

No redeemer speaks of love.

Residents of Sodom
. . . Shiftlet, Greenleaf, May.

Some are missing a part,
an arm,
or walk with a twisted foot.
If necessary, they blind themselves
to seal their tainted sight.
Country folk,
whose clothes never quite fit.

Comic grotesques
in the service of God.

She the angel with the fiery sword
striding through the city
lighting this one, that one
to a flaming illumination.

DOROTHY WALTERS

The Double Axe

With torches I have wandered the dark poppy world
Looking for Serena, my daughter with green eyes.
Wearing the colors of clouds just after sunset
She has been hidden archly in the curl of a wave.
Once, in the streets I saw her marching with men,
fifteen striding; she moved like a lily and was gone.
She has called to me with the voices of doves
And her anger, green as ice in the pale bay,
Is like a shield against the unrelenting cold.
When each morning she wakes me singing in new light
Or when I discern her far-off, bed-time moaning,
Serena with green eyes becomes all our daughters,
And on those who betray her, vested with my love,
The double axe will fall like boulders of thunder.

ANNE HAZLEWOOD-BRADY

8

We are the human beautiful who walk on water

How Beautiful You Are: 3

By love was my eye opened
so wide I drowned in light . . .

Then blue seaflowers came and filled me
and apple, quince and pear (those heavy blossoms),
and pale snowflowers, splinters of jade and coral
chipped from the bottom, the heart of the world.
For I had looked through the skin of a man's frail life,
as through his hand,
looked past his pain and his desire (as past my own)
and glimpsed the brightness behind, the wandering
    song:
stared down through our earth's tin crust to the face of
    the sun.
And gazed at the sun's face hot in the center there
so long, so straight, my gaze was blackened.

Now the pity lies open,
pity for myself and for the others,
human, brave, who know the wish to live
flowers so, only in love;
and love itself that grave
our roots must fumble open,
our loving open and live in.
We are the human beautiful
who walk on water,
striding the world-flood, disaster;

knowing well that we too carry it
lurching within our own lives—
                          and yet we come
cold with the bluefire breathing of the sea
to moisten the roots of all that will grow.

Blind, strange, singing . . .
Singing like miners under the heavy hill,
we carry ourselves for candles.

ELAINE EDELMAN

Investigation

I spoke without caring,
without hearing even.
I spoke to the dead only.
Who else?
What can the living know about war?

I said I was a conspiracy
all by myself.
They didn't believe me,
though they didn't say so.
Committees never say so
outright, it is an old custom.
But they kept showing me
rusty pictures of unattractive people
unlimited.

The committee kept asking
did I know this person
or that person,
and what did I think about them,
and what did I think about war?

I said I knew them all
through their kind introduction.
I said I would respect them
as treasures of the committee.
I said I knew the world
and should be known in return,
but as for my conspiracy,
that was my own.
I said I never met their dirty pictures.
I lied.

The dead would have known, and I spoke only to the
   dead.
I did not answer
about the war.
The committee didn't notice.
The committee wasn't pleased.
I believe they thought my responses
were either sarcastic and disrespectful
or religious and disrespectful.

They asked me who or what
I conspired against or for,
and was I known to the local police,
and was I sick or something, to waste their time like this?

I said I conspired against myself,
and was therefore an enemy

of all mankind including the committee.
I said I conspired for myself,
and was therefore an enemy
of all mankind including the committee.
I said that the local police
thought I was sick or something,
and besides they were dead, all dead.

The committee became very grave
and sent for some reporters,
and asked me did I kill them,
did I kill their police?

I said I killed my police
in my location
of myself,
during my conspiracy
of myself.
I asked the reporters
what they thought of the weather,
what they thought of the war,
and how were their children,
and I sent my love to their wives.

The dead laughed
and I was pleased.
What else is war for
but to amuse the dead?

JULIA VINOGRAD

Then and Now

In my dreams I hear my tribe
Laughing as they hunt and swim,
But dreams are shattered by rushing car,
By grinding tram and hissing train,
And I see no more my tribe of old
As I walk alone in the teeming town.

I have seen corroboree
Where that factory belches smoke;
Here where they have memorial park
One time lubras dug for yams;
One time our dark children played
There where the railway yards are now,
And where I remember the didgeridoo
Calling to us to dance and play,
Offices now, neon lights now,
Bank and shop and advertisement now,
Traffic and trade of the busy town.

No more woomera, no more boomerang,
No more playabout, no more the old ways.
Children of nature we were then,
No clocks hurrying crowds to toil.
Now I am civilized and work in the white way,
Now I have dress, now I have shoes:
"Isn't she lucky to have a good job!"
Better when I had only a dillybag.
Better when I had nothing but happiness.

KATH WALKER

12 Gates
to the City

the white man is
nocturnal that's why
he wants to get to the moon
its his rising sign

he's a vampire see
how he strikes between
dusk and dawn preying
on us day light
comes he has to be back
in his casket or office as
they call them now but
dracula would be quite comfortable

if the cracker were natural then the by
products from his body would grow
natural plants like when we are
buried flowers grow see
the stones that spring up among
their dead

nothing violates nature all
the time and even white
people came south for warmth
when the ice age hit
europe

christians should note that
it was ice water and now
fire cause the cracker is playing
with atomic matches

allah told us all
we need to know when he called
mankind hueman beings just because
they dropped the "e" the concept remains
colored cause we recognize
if we add "s" to hisstory why we ain't
a part of it or put "n" back in
demoncracy and you'll understand
the present system war
is raw any way you look
at it even with a spanish touch
and god is a dog

when the romans started counting
they started with one and went to x
an unknown mathematically speaking
so we know they couldn't deal
with twelve zodiac signs

aquarius died when
they buried atlantis this
is the age of pisces
check it out

NIKKI GIOVANNI

Provisions

What should we have taken
with us? We never could decide
on that; or what to wear,
or at what time of
year we should make this journey

so here we are, in thin
raincoats and rubber boots

on the disastrous ice, the wind rising,

nothing in our pockets

but a pencil stub, two oranges
four toronto streetcar tickets

and an elastic band, holding a bundle
of small white filing-cards
printed with important facts.

MARGARET ATWOOD

Vive Noir!

i
am going to rise
en masse
from Inner City

                    sick
                 of newyork ghettos
                chicago tenements
            l   a's slums
weary
        of exhausted lands
        sagging privies
        saying yessuh yessah
        yesSIR
        in an assortment
        of geographical dialects i
have seen my last
broken down plantation
even from a
distance
            i
will load all my goods
in '50 Chevy pickups '53
Fords fly United and '66
caddys i
        have packed in
        the old man and the old lady and
        wiped the children's noses

I'm tired
of hand me downs
shut me ups
pin me ins
keep me outs
messing me over have
just had it
baby
from
you. . . .
i'm
gonna spread out
over America
intrude
my proud blackness
all
over the place
i have wrested wheat fields
from the forests

turned rivers
from their courses

leveled mountains
at a word
festooned the land with
bridges
gemlike
on filaments of steel
moved
glistening towersofBabel in place
like blocks
sweated a whole
civilization

                    now
                           i'm
              gonna breathe fire
              through flaming nostrils BURN
                    a place for

                    me

              in the skyscrapers and the
              schoolrooms on the green
              lawns and the white
              beaches
                           i'm
              gonna wear the robes and
              sit on the benches
              make the rules and make
              the arrests say
              who can and who
              can't
                           baby you don't stand
                           a
                           chance
    i'm
         gonna put black angels
         in all the books and a black
         Christchild in Mary's arms i'm
         gonna make black bunnies black
         fairies black santas black
         nursery rhymes and
                           black

              ice cream
                           i'm
    gonna make it a
         crime

to be anything BUT   black
pass the coppertone

gonna make white
a twentyfourhour
lifetime
J.O.B.
an' when all the coppertone's gone. . . ?

MARI E. EVANS

Revolutionary Letter #19

for The Poor People's Campaign

if what you want is jobs
for everyone, you are still the enemy,
you have not thought thru, clearly
what that means

if what you want is housing,
industry
(G.E. on the Navaho
reservation)
a car for everyone, garage, refrigerator,
TV, more plumbing, scientific
freeways, you are still
the enemy, you have chosen
to sacrifice the planet for a few years of some
science fiction utopia, if what you want

still is, or can be, schools
where all our kids are pushed into one shape, are taught
it's better to be "American" than black
or Indian, or Jap, or PR, where Dick
and Jane become and are the dream, do you
look like Dick's father, don't you think your kid
secretly wishes you did

if what you want
is clinics where the AMA
can feed you pills to keep you weak, or sterile
shoot germs into your kids, while Mercke & Co
grows richer

if you want
free psychiatric help for everyone
so that the shrinks
pimps for this decadence, can make
it flower for us, if you want
if you still want a piece
a small piece of suburbia, green lawn
laid down by the square foot
color TV, whose radiant energy
kills brain cells, whose subliminal ads
brainwash your children, have taken over
your dreams

degrees from universities which are nothing
more than slum landlords, festering sinks
of lies, so you too can go forth
and lie to others on some greeny campus

THEN YOU ARE STILL
THE ENEMY, you are selling

yourself short, remember
you can have what you ask for, ask for
everything

DIANE DI PRIMA

Reciprocity

You who would sorrow even for a token
Of hurt in me no less than you would grieve
For seeing me with my whole body broken
And long no less to solace and relieve;
You who, as though you wished me mere Good Morning,
Would smash your heart upon the hardest stones
Of my distress as when you once, unscorning,
Would sleep upon the margin of my moans—
I yield my want, this house of gutted portals,
All to your want, this selfsame ravaged stack,
In testimony that between two mortals
No gift may be except a giving back.
What present could I make you from what skill
When your one need is me to need you still?

VASSAR MILLER

Lines for a Hard Time

Evil does not go always
by dark ways. On any hot
summer day, cleanshaven
it may stride across
a public place and head
purposefully for high
vantagepoints.
                    What whisper
hisses in the inner ear
take cover? Ah, and then
the boy is dead, others dead
or dying, and the evil
laps out in bits of hot
lead across the nervepools
of the nation.
                    We are sick
in our littered streets
and high places. Worms twist
in our labyrinthine skulls.
We are frightened by bland
facades.
                    The losses are always
personal. A phone rings;
a father becomes less than
the sum of his grief. Could we
say better than his own words,
And we will die as well . . .

Spiral upward into All Love?
Good man, good grieving man,
all men have lived in evil
times, though few have known it
absolutely. We persist.
We love ourselves as often
as we can. And send our sons
to walk out in open day.

GENA FORD

Letter to Robert

We who devour our unclean dead are now arisen
we are walking in the corridors under the vaulted stairs
from our shady pockets the sun has never risen
these   our vested interests   our noble heirs
in derision we have warned them
exploring with our fingers   sensing the fragile bone
who will atone for our deception?
who will consume the marrow breaking thru with a stone
listen and you will hear them the liars   the deceivers
running furtively to be alone in the shady corners
trailing their unclean fingers as they flutter up the stairs
We who devour our dead have left their prison
we have forgotten the twilight swaying about their beds
the twilight   the fiery pebbles   the livid eyes on the
    stairs
but they have resumed our wisdom

liars all & believers   they   boneless bodies dead
they have heard us groan in the corridors
they have barred the doors with threads
we who are dead have devoured us & have gathered to
    watch these children
playing games with our stones
with the polished bones of the dead
(This is what I think of the international situation—very
    lucid, is it not).

MARY FABILLI

On the Fifth Anniversary of
Bluma Sach's Death

Who knew her—
(God, all refused her!)
the Polish refugee,
caught seven times
in the Jew net?

Old
and fat
and poor.

Halls of applause
rattling
in a patched brain.

At last we met
and I wanted her
inside my door.

She came.
I poured the vermouth
of old sunrises
and said, Borrow my piano
in the mornings, Bluma.

And her arms flew,
and golden raisins
gleamed at the elbow,
and her dying skin
was heaving dough.

Done, shoulders damp,
she'd talk
beneath the parrots and swans
in the Roman garden
painted on my wall.
Wild Schumann huddled

beneath mute feathers,
ghastly parades
of brothers and children
kissed with soft beaks,
and I always said,
Tell me more!

Once the pain pushed
her to draw a line:
It is not fine of you,
she said.

We stared at wine,
and spoke no more of Poland.

In Warsaw's winter, once
she bartered, she the ripe artist
bartered her piano
for a shredding quilt.
My guilt is worse.
I handed her a sieve of hours,
and as return
peered under old leaves
at the haunted bird.

I will go into
the small black room
where my work lies scattered
and the letters on the keys
are trembling fires
and the linoleum
is a rag of ice
under my penitent feet.

But Bluma, those mornings—
how the bright rooms laughed with music
while we wept!

                VINNIE-MARIE D'AMBROSIO

The Orange Tree

Our Father, who art in Heaven,
Hallowed be thy name. Thy kingdom come,
Thy will be done, on Earth as it is in Heaven.
Give us this day our daily bread
and forgive us our Trespasses as we forgive those
who Trespass against us.
Lead us not into Temptation but deliver us from Evil
for Thine is the kingdom, the power, and the glory,
for ever and ever. Amen.
I was walking along, reciting the Lord's Prayer,
when God came down from his orange tree
and said: In the world I have tribulation,
but be of good cheer—you have overcome the world.
I asked him outright if he was on an acid trip
and he pointed out the nearest giraffe and smiled.
No, but I was, he smiled benignly.
Then would you say, I asked earnestly,
that that is the true answer? No, he smiled
patiently. Your trip was from darkness into light.
I cried then, for he had hit upon the crux of the matter.
Oh God, I said. Call me Man, he interrupted.
Oh Man, I corrected myself, Where has my light gone?
I've misplaced it. At this he shinnied back up
into his orange tree. His message was clear.
I started taking Vitamin C enriched pills and one day
God rode by on a Honda. I hailed him for a ride
but he said he only had an hour to get to the war

and had to stop at the Internal Revenue office
on the way. I shrugged. I guess
I don't always understand his business.

ELLEN PEARCE

Crystal

My face is black. See the moon? My eyes.
How distant from you I am. No; I'm
the inside of your sleep, your mouth
chewing food, your ancestors coming from their
photographs
at night in the shape of animals, in the shape of
two moons, watching.

Whose name are you? Whose face? You are this
paper before one word comes to it, the hole in life
death makes, plaster figures—unpainted.
Christ stands on the wall behind you, the father-mother
tree, the
perpetual ghost man. Everything becomes a lie,
this poem

becomes a lie, my face—the one on the outside, the one
you think you see, the one making words—becomes
a lie, becomes a way of filling
your bones with explosives, with the dark, strange
water of the moon.

FAYE KICKNOSWAY

The Traveling Out

I wonder, since we are both travelling out,
If we may go together? Thank you.

You may be sure you will be alone
And private as though I were no one.
God knows, I do not wish to increase your burden.
Naturally, these airports, blinding cities,
And foundry lights confuse you, make you
More solitary than the sight of one lost lamp
Across a bare land promising life there—
Someone over that field alone and perhaps
Waiting for you. That used to be the way.

Feel perfectly free to choose how
You will be alone, since we are going together.
Of course, I never move, I merely hold you
In my mind like a prayer. You are my way
Of praying, and I have chosen you out of hordes
Of travellers to speak to silently, on my own.
I will be with you, with your baffled anger
Among fuming cities, with your grief
At having lost dark fields and lamplight.
It is my way of moving, or praying—

Oh, not to give you someone like me,
That's all over, impossible, I go nowhere;
And besides, nothing is given, absolutely

Nothing and no one, only white sermons among
The white of a billion bulbs. No,
Sitting here behind my shutters at twilight,
I am stretching over the blazing lanes,
The dazed crowds jostled and razed
By light, only to join your mind and guide you
Gently, leading you, not, alas, to my own lamp
Across the fields of the world, or to a cozy last
Prayer of lamplight blessing the fields of the air,
But out into hordes of stars that move away
As we move, and for which your travelling
Prepares you to go out a little more boldly,
All alone as I am alone.

LUCILE ADLER

Nightbreak

Something broken   Something
I need   By someone
I love   Next year
will I remember what
This anger   unreal
                    yet
has to be gone through
The sun to set
on this anger
                I go on
head down   into it
The mountain pulsing

Into the oildrum   drops
the ball of fire.

Time is quiet   doesn't break things
or even wound   Things are in danger
from people   The frail clay lamps
of Mesopotamia
row on row under glass
in the ethnological section
little hollows for dried-
up oil   The refugees
with their identical
tales of escape   I don't
collect what I can't use   I need
what can be broken.

In the bed the pieces fly together
and the rifts fill   or else
my body is a list   of wounds
symmetrically placed
a village
blown open   by planes
that did not   finish the job
The enemy has   withdrawn
between raids   become invisible
there are
               no agencies
                          of relief
the darkness becomes utter
Sleep   cracked and flaking
sifts over the shaken   target

What breaks   is night
not day   The white

scar   splitting
over the east
The crack weeping
Time for the pieces
                to move
dumbly back
          toward each other.

ADRIENNE RICH

The Old One and
the Wind

She loves the wind.
There on the edge of the known world, at ninety,
In her tall house, any wildness in the elements
Is as welcome as an old friend.
When the surgically patched elms and sycamores
Crack off their heavy limbs in the freak snow storm
Of October, she rejoices; the massy hail
That drives craters into her groomed lawn
Stirs her sluggish heart to a riot of beating.

A cluster of cottonwood trees in the swale
Of the prairie, oasis now in a desert of wheat fields,
Is all that is left of the home place. No one
Is left to remember the days there with her:
The playhouse sheltered behind the cowshed,
The whirlwinds that made a column of corn shucks,

Winters when snow brushed out all the fences,
Springs when the white of the snow turned to daisies,
Wind-bent as were the urchins who picked them.

To her in her tall house in the tame town, the wind
That escapes the windbreaks of man's constructing
Blows from a distance beyond the young's conceiving,
Is rife with excitements of the world's beginning
And its end.

CLARICE SHORT

9
I was born awake

Rino's Song

I was born conscious, I can't remember
a time of not being lucid,
a moment without cynicism,
yanking the electric bell in my crib,
averting mouth from spoiled milk:
this was no consciousness of reality
(reality eluded even then), but rather—
consciousness of consciousness. Memories!
I have them from the very beginning,
the fact that I was an abortion, for example, born dark,
    tiny, and shriveled.

Two more months, and an Aryan he-man
like my three brothers, large and healthy. But they
    exhaust me,
the thoughts from three months on. . . .
Pain is only being born awake.

LYNNE LAWNER

More Clues

Mother, because you never spoke to me
I go my life, do I, searching in women's faces
the lost word, a word in the shape of a breast?

Father, because both of you never touched me
do I search for men building space on space?
There was no touch, both my hands bandaged close.

I come from that, but I come far, to touch to word.
Can they reach me now, or inside out in a universe
of touch, of speech is it? somewhere in me, clues?

MURIEL RUKEYSER

The Triple Mirror

What did you think when first
as a child
you met yourself in vanity's mirror
subdivided by three?

Id, ego, superego,
did you fathom their names?
Or didn't your trinity matter?

Leafed in the glass like pressed clover;
stared at with awe equal to your own;
the burgeoning godhead of your imperfection;
how did you impress you?

I remember I laughed;
delightedly hiding and seeking,
teasing from depths of unknowing
my triple declension,
peer more than, then, I suspected.

Self awareness takes time.
I have had it. Now in
life's looking glass,
wwhen wrung round by
three-person me, I bow.

My familiars, they nod.
Silence the even exchange of
the guilty.

GLORIA ODEN

In the Field

My name is Phyllis Janik.
I'm 25 and you like the way I look
at things. So I say,
let today be a day
for nothing, wasted on

love or long walks
or some imagined saga,
small adventure at coffee.
Here the circles
I try to say myself in
come out lines,
and someone is bound to question
my title.

It would seem
this is the season
for the genuinely marvelous,
for Man the writer or hunter,
and I will acknowledge
a certain feminine failure
in the field.
       But sometimes
outside this wide glass
it seems as though
the sleek cats stalk. It's then
I see the roles reversed
and they're all home
while I'm out hunting tigers—
not for dinner, just for tigers.

PHYLLIS JANIK

Let us suppose the mind
to be a reversible tea-kettle
    NO
rather, let us assume it
as being a coil of electricity
which, when provoked (say by Spring-dawn)
will extend an outer portion of itself

as a moth would extend
its furry antennae, its white feeler
to examine the light
coiling about the rim of a silver bowl.

Perhaps this
is the Superb Reality/Mind
being a coil of electricity,

able to extend
—thereby
proclaiming the outer worlds
comparable animation to be
(in that its substance is critically crystal)
Reflector . . .
    of the soul . . .

Notice the moth. pale creature
whose frail tissue wings flutter
a purple vibrancy (nervous!) of soul
when, extending its antennae it discovers
not god
    but its own miracle.

BARBARA MORAFF

Cinéma Vérité

This road is so fuzzy
it is sometimes hard to know
whether we are moving
or it is moving under us,
the scenery jerked along behind
like the sets of an old movie:
Time Passes.

Obviously, we are dressed for a journey.
The crude map is in our fist.
The air is heavy, like water.
Forms sometimes flash by like fishes,
too fast to tell whether they are
other travelers heading toward a common destination,
or aborted versions of ourself
that somehow floated free
in an earlier episode.

Before, there was sequence and measure.
A small fist unrolled to a recognizable hand,
blooded and veined.
Spring was to the right,
while on the left
snow crusted the curling branches,
winter always coming on.

Here, all things reflect each other.

The sun scorches the night sky.
The old man playing the organ in the country church
is also the girl strolling in the garden.
Mixed twins wander in circles overhead,
arm in arm,
but you cannot tell the female from the male.
Nearby, a body thuds heavily down,
a corpse imprinting the dust.
Instantly, a thousand roses spring from his brow.

You watch unmoved.
You cannot say if your composure
is the calm of acceptance or the mask of a dulled heart.

You move on,
muttering old benedictions
as you go.

DOROTHY WALTERS

Running Through Sleep

I would prefer to live quietly in silks,
Like a lady, in a place where a lady lives,
But I have seen this body I carry around alone;
Streamlined for sleep, its arms, ears, and lips removed,
It resembles a fish swimming through dark water,
Or a fire burning undetected,
Watching everything around it
Turn to soft, wet ash;

It runs faster as the light approaches
Along the edges of its skin,
It tries to recall the shape of a foot,
Or a face smiling in a photograph,
Something it can fit into
So it won't disappear

Sometimes it's no more than a dampness
On the undersides of logs and rocks,
Running without a trace into the earth,
And the roots of plants;
But at night the shoes of people with the sweetest
    laughter,
The gentlest step,
Are shoes with knives in the soles
That can cut three feet deep,
And the heart seeks refuge
In the oldest, smoothest stones

Sometimes it feels like the water forming in clouds,
Commanding a view of whole sides of continents,
And the ocean's edge;
But it fears falling from such a height
And having no place to go;
It fears that the police will find it rummaging
Through someone else's closet,
Stuffing its heart with rags

KATHLEEN NORRIS

The Importance of Mirrors

The woman in her room is standing at the mirror.
What is she seeing? The way the wind tears her hair
As it blows through the window? No. Does she hear
Something? The cry of the old hen in the yard

Like all of them out there, from wedding card
To chopping-block, dust on their wings endured
From the leaping roosters? No. She has not heard.
Well, do her white nostrils then catch the scent

From the bedpost behind her exuding faint,
(It's a virgin's cot, originally meant
For a maidenhead's taking, its boards felled luxuriant
With flowers and bees)? Does she smell it? No, nor taste

Nor feel what's physically about. She has no age, is lost
In the glass, where all her years has querying gazed
At child or wife or hag. She is the host,
Herself her guest. The mirror is her open door.

HELGA SANDBURG

Encounter

What cry was that
   zeroed rose-color,
   bending from great
   distance, sudden
   like a sun-spoke
   straight
   and curved to wrap me
   in bright light,
   blinding my breath?

You were there
   and took my eyes deep,
   drowning the surfaces
   we swam in.

Am I freed or bound now
   by a cry that dives
   back into silence?

      Both.

GERALDINE HAMMOND

Town I Left

In that town were hard spaces
of no trees growing, a sky
I wore on my head like a tin
wash basin, noon
a bleaching wind,
the land bleached
and I, too, lost all color.

Some say the young look on death
quickly and then away. Perhaps.
I only know in that town
I was young and I looked full
in death's stiffening face,
I heard its voice
selling shoes and rice and bricks,
I heard it in chains of porch swings
rusting the winter winds,
its cough from crows
in the cottonwoods,
among people sucked too dry
by their own all-day dying
to care about mine.

HELEN SORRELLS

I've been going around everywhere without any skin
     And it hurts. The wind hurts. Any touch.
     Attitudes distant from my own look out and find me.
     When I see a face a long way off, my forehead blisters.
     Raw the hot flesh under skin.

     Now I am going to live so deep down in
     That my skin will be a lost harm like Algeria.
     Down in will be craters, violences to be tolerated
     By other violences. Not by you,
     Not by country or climate, this personal flaying.

                                          JOSEPHINE MILES

Palindrome

"There is less difficulty—indeed, no logical difficulty
at all—in imagining two portions of the universe, say
two galaxies, in which time goes one way in one galaxy,
and the opposite way in the other. . . . Intelligent
beings in each galaxy would regard their own time as
'forward' and time in the other galaxy as 'backward.' "
          MARTIN GARDNER, in *Scientific American*

Somewhere now she takes off the dress I am putting
on. It is evening in the anti-world, where she lives.
She is forty-five years away from her death, the hole
which spit her out into pain, impossible at first,

later easing, going, gone. She has unlearned much
by now. Her skin is firming, her memory sharpens,
her hair has grown glossy. She sees without glasses;
she falls in love easily. Her husband has lost his
shuffle; they laugh together. Their money shrinks,
but their ardor increases. Soon her second child
will be young enough to fight its way into her
body and change its life to monkey to frog to
tadpole to cluster of cells to tiny island
to nothing. She is making a list:

Things I will need in the past
   lipstick
   shampoo
   transistor radio
   Sergeant Pepper
   gel for blackheads
   5-year diary with lock

She is eager, having heard about
adolescent love and the freedom of
children. She wants to read *Crime and
Punishment* and ride on a roller-coaster
without getting sick. I think of her, as
she will be at fifteen, awkward, too serious.
In the mirror I see she uses her left hand to
write, her other to open a jar. By now our lives
should have crossed. Somewhere sometime we must
   have
passed one another like going and coming trains,
with both of us looking the other way.

LISEL MUELLER

song of the strange young duckling

so i cut my hair; so i'm shorn
long locks fallen down—a disowned rapunzel,
or a plucked goose. well,

beauty's ephemeral stuff
and i never had it anyway:
but don't let anybody tell you
that i'm not singing.

so i washed off the paints, lovely spells
that kept me fresh and young; young.
i'm a lined old lady, i'm a baker's dozen,
old bunwoman singing:

don't let anyone come on like
prince or a princess; swansdown, ah, it stains
like tints and grease in goosefeather beds.

they've been sleeping too long
and it's time—
trim them, wash them, pluck the quills out!

out of the nest. don't let them tell you
you'll be dead and gone. i tell you. you're singing.

DEBORAH MUNRO

10

Only where there is language
is there world

The Demon Lover

Fatigue, regrets. The lights
go out in the parking lot
two by two. Snow blindness
settles over the suburb.
Desire. Desire. The nebula
opens in space, unseen,
your heart utters its great beats
in solitude. A new
era is coming in.
Gauche as we are, it seems
we have to play our part.

A plaid dress, silk scarf,
and eyes that go on stinging.
Woman, stand off. The air
glistens like silk.
She's gone. In her place stands
a schoolgirl, morning light,
the half-grown bones
of innocence. Is she
your daughter or your muse,
this tree of blondness
grown up in a field of thorns?

Something piercing and marred.
Take note. Look back. When quick
the whole northeast went black

and prisoners howled and children
ran through the night with candles,
who stood off motionless
side by side while the moon swam up
over the drowned houses?
Who neither touched nor spoke?
whose nape, whose finger-ends
nervelessly lied the hours away?

A voice presses at me.
If I give in it won't
be like the girl the bull rode,
all Rubens flesh and happy moans.
But to be wrestled like a boy
with tongue, hips, knees, nerves, brain . . .
with language?
He doesn't know. He's watching
breasts under a striped blouse,
his bull's head down. The old
wine pours again through my veins.

Goodnight, then. 'Night. Again
we turn our backs and weary
weary we let down.
Things take us hard, no question.
How do you make it, all the way
from here to morning? I touch
you, made of such nerve
and flare and pride and swallowed tears.
Go home. Come to bed. The skies
look in at us, stern.
And this is an old story.

I dreamed about the war.

We were all sitting at table
in a kitchen in Chicago.
The radio had just screamed
that Illinois was the target.
No one felt like leaving,
we sat by the open window
and talked in the sunset.
I'll tell you that joke tomorrow,
you said with your saddest smile,
if I can remember.

The end is just a straw,
a feather furling slowly down,
floating to light by chance, a breath
on the long-loaded scales.
Posterity trembles like a leaf
and we go on making heirs and heirlooms.
The world, we have to make it,
my coexistent friend said, leaning
back in his cell.
Siberia vastly hulks
behind him, which he did not make.

Oh futile tenderness
of touch in a world like this!
how much longer, dear child,
do you think sex will matter?
There might have been a wedding
that never was:
two creatures sprung free
from castiron covenants.
Instead our hands and minds
erotically waver . . .
Lightness is unavailing.

Catalpas wave and spill
their dull strings across this murk of spring.
I ache, brilliantly.
Only where there is language is there world.
In the harp of my hair, compose me
a song. Death's in the air,
we all know that. Still, for an hour,
I'd like to be gay. How could a gay song go?
Why that's your secret, and it shall be mine.
We are our words, and black and bruised and blue.
Under our skins, we're laughing.

In triste veritas?
Take hold, sweet hands, come on. . . .
Broken!
When you falter, all eludes.
This is a seasick way,
this almost/never touching, this
drawing-off, this to-and-fro.
Subtlety stalks in your eyes,
your tongue knows what it knows.
I want your secrets—I *will* have them out.
Seasick, I drop into the sea.

ADRIENNE RICH

Myth

Long afterward, Oedipus, old and blinded, walked the
roads.   He smelled a familiar smell.   It was
the Sphinx.   Oedipus said, "I want to ask one ques-
    tion.
Why didn't I recognize my mother?"   "You gave the
wrong answer," said the Sphinx.   "But that was what
made everything possible," said Oedipus.   "No," she
    said.
"When I asked, What walks on four legs in the morning,
two at noon, and three in the evening, you answered,
Man.   You didn't say anything about woman."
"When you say Man," said Oedipus, "you include women
too. Everyone knows that."   She said, "That's what
you think."

MURIEL RUKEYSER

The Voices Inescapable

We are never free of the voices.
On waves and wires
Out of the clouds they speak to us.
Wood and steel, nails, bring them through walls.

Edging all buildings, voices mumble their pitch and
    pause.

Yet down over the rocks of this land
in the undercurrents of the sea
The others are not silent,
Gull and dove,
The coyote over the hills
At night gives us his cry.
Listen to the small voices of the drops of rain now
Settling over us.
The shell whispers back our blood.
The owl tells us at night
Of the soft passers in the leaves.
And the voices from the cloud
Cry: there is no other way.

We will call with the rest for mercy
When the blood
Bludgeons on the carpet,
With the hawk's rabbit
And the raped girl in the forest.

ANN STANFORD

modern poetry

tomorrow morning, some poet will wake up
to find himself famous
for writing a novel, for posing
nude in the centerfold of a magazine, for

leading a political movement,
for killing his wife.
it will not be for having
written a poem.
or perhaps he will not wake up at all.
think of Hart Crane who,
sailing north on a steamer from Mexico,
drank his way over the side
of the S.S. *Orizaba*
and Sylvia, trying to deal with
what most of us cannot accept, sticking
her head in the oven
one English morning
or even Frank O'Hara,
killed by a dune buggy on Fire Island
it is these fine details of the departure
or the eccentricities of existence
which catch in the public memory,
bright fringe from the hem of the fabric
snagged by the rough edges
of curiosity,
not the risks, the bravery
of this murderous art,
the challenge of the line, not even the title
of a single poem.

ANITA SKEEN

Lines for Those
to Whom Tragedy Is Denied

These women have no language and so they chatter
In the rhythm of stereotype that is won
After certain years and certain money.
Or perhaps they once rose naked from the sea
And the stereotype rose from them like a snapshot
Snapped by envious fingers, an act of love
They never noticed.
The ladies are metronomes or pendulums
As their laments swing from one to the other
Around the heavy oak table, rooted to the floor
Like many another oak: here the roots are bolts.
The floor is parquet, polished and indifferent
To the tappings of expensive feet.
No matter what these ladies say, no matter,
It is crime to listen to the language of ladies
Who have no language.

> *Fifteen years ago when we were first married*
> *we lived on an army base; we had no money;*
> *we saved to go to the camp movies, which cost*
> *a dime. We saved all week . . . for the movies.*

The army has cleared out, marched away, the soldiers
  are
Grown out of their boys' uniforms and some are
Rotted entirely out of them and some, like your hus-
  bands,

Are important now and very expensive.

> *The car broke down in Kansas City, on our*
> *way to his mother in Texas. And I broke*
> *down, with the baby and all, and he sat*
> *talking to me and kidding in the car, in*
> *the rain . . . in Kansas City. . . . That was*
> *nineteen years ago.*

Of sorrow their diamonds are stereotypes, again,
And no tears can quite equal their brilliance.
Bloated out of themselves like corpses in water
Such suburban ladies stare upon their former bodies,
Girls' bodies, and it is the innocence of plant and algae
They seem to taste, and not human guise.

> *Then Michael was born, and then I got*
> > *pregnant*
> *again and we were afraid to write home;*
> *between his family and mine what choice did*
> *we have? I had the baby, that's Perry at*
> *Yale. He's going to Italy this summer. . . .*

There are five ladies here and two are divorced and
Sad to say divorce awaits the others, like death.
Their husbands never dream away time in Kansas City.
Never do they dream of khaki and mud and never youth
Without power, never the submersion in shapes
Unshaped like the good silky leather gloves
Tangled around the straps of leather purses.
Their husbands account for the success of airlines
And the thick red carpets of certain restaurants.
Ah, manly men!—and stripped clean of the garments
Of tawdry questions: What am I?
The latest light-toned lipstick cannot quite disguise
The bitter bitter set of your skulls' teeth, ladies.
And you are educated, or were.
Your milk-curdled glands stir

At the fate of adolescent children, your children,
Who will not obey. No fur to your bodies, ladies,
But the pelts of animals killed for you.
These pelts gleam and glisten
In the five o'clock light of the Oak Room
Of the club. We are very wealthy here and
Very liberal about Negroes.

> *We never argued, never fought.*
> *Then that night he told me, before*
> *guests, that the house was sold; he*
> *said, "Your taste was never good."*
> *It seemed to begin then. . . .*

In the depths of the table over which they lean
Their younger selves dream and drown
And the gold of their trinkets which is real
And heartbreaking in beauty, and the pink
Of their gentle besieged ears, and the perfumed wires
They wear as hair, and the droning question of
Their chatter grow heavy, heavy
In the absence of men and the absence of sky and
Cloudy wet mornings in other cities, minor cities,
And the rapid jerky heartbeat of youth with no
Gold to it but youth.
Do the ribbed wonders of the brain still hold
In terraces without nerves the outlines
Of faces, of love? And what was love? And who were
Those boy husbands, those wives; and who were those
    babies
So loved and feared? When they were real were they
    real?
Now it is certain that the time of day is real.
The table, the floor, the panelled walls are real
And real the density of bodies and
The images, like angels, of ladies settled and bizarre

As certain birds bred for color and song and beyond
Their youth's charm.

JOYCE CAROL OATES

The Dictionary is
an *His*torian

A Found Political Poem

Woman, women
1.   An adult female person, as distinguished from a
man or child; sometimes, any female person, often as
disting. from *lady* (sense 7).

> *Women* are soft, mild, pitiful, and flexible. *Shak.*
> And the rib, which the Lord God had taken
>   from man, made he a *woman.*
> Gen. ii. 22.

2.   The typical member of the female sex; used as a
generic singular without an article; the female part of
the human race; womankind.

> Man is destined to be a prey to *woman. Thackeray.*

3.   With *the.* Distinctively feminine nature, qualities,
characteristics, or disposition; womanhood; womanli-
ness; as, subduing the *woman* in her; sometimes in the
phrase *the woman of it*, the characteristically feminine
factor, action, response, reaction, or the like.
4.   A female attendant or servant.
5.   *a* A paramour; mistress. *b pl.* Females as partners

in sexual intercourse or irregularities; as, to refrain
from *women*.
6.   A wife. *Familiar*.
7.   A female person of a position, calling, or standing,
specified in a phrase with *of* (sense 15); as, a *woman* of
breeding, of color, of title; a *woman* of all work, of
letters; the *woman* of the house; often in contemptuous
epithets connoting easy virtue; as, a *woman* of plea-
sure, of the town, of the streets.
8.   The reverse of a coin, originally as bearing figure
of Britannia. *Brit.*
9.   Bringer of woe; by whimsical etymological deriva-
tion from *woe + man*. *Obs.*

JUDITH McCOMBS

Falling Out

—tight,—proof, unavailable
in our capsule and turned off
to communiqués, we orbited
until our unit came apart, until

the old pull re-exerts.
I spill,
susceptible, in the human air.
Moving among bodies, bombarded with messages
already I commit it all, more
than could happen, turning historical
with strangers, living with passers-

by. Outside the gemini kingdom
people are catching.

HELEN CHASIN

Signature

If I sing because I must
being made of singing dust,

and I cry because of need
being born of watered seed,

and I grow like twisted tree
having neither symmetry

nor the structure to avert
the falling axe, the minor hurt,

yet of one thing I am sure
that this bears my signature,

that I knew love when it came
and I called it by its name.

HANNAH KAHN

The Turtle's Belly

I will not be inhabited.
I will know nothing but storms and fishes. Death will not
touch my shores in the form of man or poetry.
I am omnipotent and the rocks and reefs will perpetuate
    me.

Within the mist which has not deserted the island this
    century
is an unsuspected wealth of life that would make the
    mountain
shudder in revulsion. Even the creatures that dwell there
believe they live in ultimate solitude
for the unmelodic calls and twitterings of unseen birds
are the only things which punctuate the silence.
One man stole onto this desolate land when the seas
were sleeping and has lived there inconspicuously
for forgotten months. He rowed a thousand miles
from the Sacramento Valley in a single day, alone and
working hard at the oars. Once the mainland was out of
    sight
everything was gray and uniform and time stopped its
aimless pacing. An occasional dolphin cut through the
    water
alongside but the waves rolled away any foam trace.
Then Kiska stood imperiously on the sea before him and
the little man scrambled up her banks, exchanging
    glances

with a pelagic cormorant, though he didn't know it.
From then on he was anonymous, even to himself.
He had fed his vocabulary to the gull on the way, to
become
a wandering lupine. Without the volcano he was the
highest ground,
never looking to see himself dancing through the grass
and sky.
He made passion without his body or anything it had
contained.
Now, he didn't think; he had lost the context of thought.
He was nothing he had ever been and existed not
knowing how to do so.

Ellen Pearce

Walking the Beach

Branches ripped by a storm tide
Drift in the shallows where they fell
Away, their light limbs wavering
In the current's pull. Nearby
Two lovers' spendthrift bodies lie
Stripped to the August sun. The lovers
Fell away, they sleep in a light embrace
Indifferent to the sun and tide.

Adrift in sleep, their dreaming flesh
Casts everything away but touch, oblivious
Of the pensive walkers by the shore

And the cries of children, the luminous
Scattered sea-gifts riddling the sand.
Beyond the glittering tide-wrack beach
Some creature on the waste sea-floor
Is spinning a heavenly city
From its dreaming shell.

SARAH YOUNGBLOOD

Portrait of an Artist

For dear life some do
Many a hard thing,
Train the meticulous mind
Upon meaning, seek
And find, and yet discard
All that is not of reality's tough rind.

A cool divining rod,
The heart, another tool,
Keen as a hawk's eye,
Supple as water, bends
Responsive to all four
Humors. In many sympathy runs dry

Or blots and blurs. To be
Ascetic for life's sake,
Honest and passionate,
Is rare. I think of those

Images of Buddha placed
In shells, and later found encased in pearl.

BARBARA HOWES

Singing Aloud

We all have our faults. Mine is trying to write poems.
New scenery, someone I like, anything sets me off!
I hear my own voice going on, like a god or an oracle,
That cello-tone, intuition. That bell-note of wisdom!

And I can't get rid of the tempting tic of pentameter,
Of the urge to impose a form on what I don't under-
    stand,
Or that which I have to transform because it's too grim as
    it is.
But age is improving me: Now, when I finish a poem

I no longer rush out to impose it on friendly colleagues.
I climb through the park to the reservoir, peer down at
    my own reflection,
Shake a blossoming branch so I am covered with petals,
Each petal a metaphor. . . .

By the time we reach middle life, we've all been deserted
    and robbed.
But flowers and grass and animals keep me warm.
And I remind myself to become philosophic:
We are meant to be stripped down, to prepare us for
    something better.

And, often, I sing aloud. As I grow older
I give way to innocent folly more and more often.
The squirrels and rabbits chime in with inaudible voices.
I feel sure that the birds make an effort to be antiphonal.

When I go to the zoo, the primates and I, in communion,
Hoot at each other, or signal with earthy gestures.
We must move further out of town, we musical birds and
   animals,
Or they'll lock us up like the apes, and control us forever.

CAROLYN KIZER

Two Roads, Etc.

for Carolyn Kizer

Here I am,
Novice of many years,
Still writing poems
Full of betrayal and lost love,
Forever turning the events of my life
In my hand
Like a strange stone
To be examined in the light
Of Tragedy.

She, meanwhile,
With a shrug of one shoulder,
Says,

"By the time we reach middle life,
We've all been deserted and robbed,"
And goes on to the next stanza.

Well, none would dispute her.
But to take the news so calmly.
To let go the bar
And go whizzing through space
Humming a little tune to oneself.

True, she's lived deep:
Slept with famous poets,
Brows and all,
Got divorced once or twice,
Was rejoiced at seeing afar
The naked genitals of Chinese laborers
When she was "very young."

When I was very young,
I scanned the diagrams
Of ancient medical texts.
And was properly shaken.
Poets were names in books,
Their brows the windy heights,
Unscaled, of accompanying illustrations.
In that country, life was real
Only the way a poem is real
When it is about to be written.

Merwin said: "This way the dust,
That way the dust,"
And Yeats, earlier,
"Everything we look upon is blest,"
Both, of course, being perfectly correct.

DOROTHY WALTERS

At the Western Shore

Still, after all, the kelp remain,
Floating in dreams, inescapable,
Obscene.   I would remember shells
And the moon, sea-moss, starfish,
Delicate-colored rocks, the finished
Gifts of the sea, and must contend with these
Unfinished things: the cast remnants
Of a fecund sea, uprooted phalloi flung
On the salt sand, emblems of a failed
Power of life.

             It is the listlessness
Of time and space they take for home,
Having no roots, that ravels sleep—
Drifting upon the beaches of the world
To rot, or tossed to sea again in the ebb
Pull of the indifferent tide.

Who would have guessed the rose
Has such tenacious roots?   The moon
For all its shiftings holds the sea
In place.   Even the moss grows old
Upon the shallowest rocks.

SARAH YOUNGBLOOD

Matins

1.

The authentic! Shadows of it
sweep past in dreams, one could say imprecisely,
evoking the almost-silent
ripping apart of giant
sheets of cellophane. No.
It thrusts up close. Exactly in dreams
it has you off-guard, you
recognize it before you have time.
For a second before waking
the alarm bell is a red conical hat, it
takes form.

2.

The authentic! I said
rising from the toilet seat.
The radiator in rhythmic knockings
spoke of the rising steam.
The authentic, I said
breaking the handle of my hairbrush as I
brushed my hair in
rhythmic strokes: That's it,
that's joy, it's always
a recognition, the known
appearing fully itself, and
more itself than one knew.

3.

The new day rises
as heat rises,
knocking in the pipes
with rhythms it seizes for its own
to speak of its invention—
the real, the new-laid
egg whose speckled shell
the poet fondles and must break
if he will be nourished.

4.

A shadow painted where
yes, a shadow must fall.
The cow's breath
not forgotten in the mist, in the
words. Yes,
verisimilitude draws up
heat in us, zest
to follow through,
follow through,
follow
transformations of day
in its turning, in its becoming.

5.

Stir the holy grains, set
the bowls on the table and
call the child to eat.

While we eat we think,
as we think an undercurrent
of dream runs through us
faster than thought
towards recognition.

Call the child to eat,
send him off, his mouth
tasting of toothpaste, to go down
into the ground, into a roaring train
and to school.

His cheeks are pink
his black eyes hold his dreams, he has left
forgetting his glasses.

Follow down the stairs at a clatter
to give them to him and save
his clear sight.

Cold air
comes in at the street door.

  6.
The authentic! It rolls
just out of reach, beyond
running feet and
stretching fingers, down
the green slope and into
the black waves of the sea.
Speak to me, little horse, beloved,
tell me
how to follow the iron ball,
how to follow through to the country
beneath the waves
to the place where I must kill you and you step out
of your bones and flystrewn meat
tall, smiling, renewed,
formed in your own likeness.

7.
Marvelous Truth, confront us
at every turn,
in every guise, iron ball,
egg, dark horse, shadow,
cloud
of breath on the air,

dwell
in our crowded hearts
our steaming bathrooms, kitchens full of
things to be done, the
ordinary streets.

Thrust close your smile
that we know you, terrible joy.

DENISE LEVERTOV

BIOGRAPHIES OF THE POETS

Lucile Adler lives with her family in Santa Fe, New Mexico. Her poems have appeared in *The New Mexico Quarterly, Puerta del Sol, The Desert Review, Poetry, The Nation, The New Yorker, Poetry Northwest*, other periodicals, and several anthologies. Two books, *The Traveling Out* and *The Society of Anna*, include selections of her work. Ms. Adler has just completed a new manuscript.

alta, born in 1942, currently lives in California with her two daughters. She is founder and director of the Shameless Hussy Press, which publishes women's writing, and has edited an anthology of poetry by women, *Remember Our Fire*. Her books include *Freedom's in Sight, Letters to Women, Song of the Wife/Song of the Mistress, No Visible Means of Support, Poems and Prose, Burn This and Memorize Yourself*, and *I Am Not a Practicing Angel*.

Maya Angelou is the author of *I Know Why the Caged Bird Sings, Gather Together in my Name*, and *Just Give Me a Cool Drink of Water 'fore I Diiie*. She toured Europe and Africa for the State Department in *Porgy and Bess* and has taught dance in Rome and Tel Aviv. While in Africa she was on the faculty of the University of Ghana and wrote for the local newspapers. Other credits include work in the theater, television, and film. She is currently living in Sonoma, California, and her latest book of poetry is *Oh Pray My Wings Are Gonna Fit Me Well*.

Lila Arnold was born on a farm, and except for several years in England has spent most of her life in the Midwest. She lives in Wichita, Kansas, with her husband, an attorney, and their three children. A social worker with interests in traveling and treasure hunting, Lila Arnold is also accumulating hours toward an M.F.A. in creative writing. Her poetry has appeared in several small journals.

Margaret Atwood was born in Canada in 1939, where she now resides. She has written two novels, *The Edible Woman* and *Surfacing*, and has published a nonfiction work, *Survival: A Thematic Guide to Canadian Literature*. Her poems have appeared in *The New Yorker, The Atlantic Monthly, Poetry*, and *Mademoiselle*. She has published several books of poetry, of which *The Circle Game* received the Governor-General's Award in 1966.

Phyllis Beauvais was born in Gering, Nebraska, in 1940. Her education encompasses a B.A. from Loretto Heights College, an M.A. from San Francisco State College, and a Ph.D. from Hartford Seminary. She has held jobs as a balloon salesman, a quiltmaker, a migrant laborer, and a waitress. Now, after many years of adventuring, she has settled down happily with her husband and two children in Litchfield, Connecticut, where she is a psychotherapist working mostly with women through dreams and expressive meditation.

Louise Bogan was born in 1897 in Livermore Falls, Maine, of Irish parents. Her books include *Body of This Death*, *Dark Summer*, *The Sleeping Fury*, *Poems and New Poems*, and *The Blue Estuaries*. She won numerous awards from *Poetry* magazine, and her *Collected Poems, 1923-1953*, won the Bollingen Prize in Poetry, 1954. She contributed a volume on the history of American poetry from 1900 to 1950 to the *Twentieth-Century Literature in America* series and became known for the poetry criticism she wrote for *The New Yorker* magazine.

besmilr brigham was born September 29, 1923, in Pace, Mississippi. Her poetry has appeared in many anthologies and in her book, *Heaved from the Earth*. Of her published work, Ms. brigham writes: "[it] is like what one sees of an iceberg; and as I go on living, more amasses."

Gwendolyn Brooks was born in Topeka, Kansas, in 1917, but was raised in Chicago, where she attended Wilson Junior College. She won the Pulitzer Prize for Poetry in 1950 for *Annie Allen* and is the author of a novel, *Maud Martha*, and a book of poems for young readers, *The Bean Eaters*. Ms. Brooks is Poet Laureate of Illinois, and lives with her husband and two children in Chicago, where she teaches poetry at Northeastern Illinois State College, Columbia College, and Elmhurst College.

Rita Mae Brown was born November 28, 1944. Orphaned and adopted at an early age, she now lives and writes in Boston. She has written the novels *Rubyfruit Jungle* and *In Her Day*. Her volumes of poetry are *The Hand That Cradles the Rock* and *Songs to a Handsome Woman*. Her collected political essays are forthcoming under the title *The Plain Brown Rapper*.

Lynne Butler was born in Hays, Kansas, in 1943 and still considers herself a midwesterner although she now lives in Alabama. She received an M.F.A. from the University of Arkansas and has taught at

Wichita State University and the University of North Alabama. Her work has appeared in various small magazines and anthologies. She is married and has a son.

Jane Chambers has been published in *The Ladder*.

Helen Chasin is the author of *Coming Close* and *Casting Stones*, and her work has appeared in various periodicals and anthologies. Formerly a Radcliffe Institute Fellow and a Visiting Lecturer at the Iowa Writers' Workshop, she is a 1976 recipient of a Creative Artists Public Service grant and is Writer-in-Residence (Poetry) of The Writers Community. She lives in New York City.

Laura Chester was born April 13, 1949, and grew up in Milwaukee and Wisconsin. *The All Night Salt Lick*, a book of poems coauthored with her husband, poet Geoffrey Young, was written while traveling in Africa. Other books include *Tiny Talk*, *Chunk Off And Float*, and *Rising Tides*, an anthology she coedited. A winner of the Stelhoff Poetry Prize, Ms. Chester helps edit *Best Friends* and *Stooge*.

Jane Cooper was born in Atlantic City, New Jersey, in 1924. Since the age of twenty-five she has been deeply involved in teaching, and writes that teaching brought her back to poetry through a different door. In 1968 her first published book, *The Weather of Six Mornings*, was the Lamont Selection of the Academy of American Poets. She has held grants from the Ingram Merrill and Guggenheim foundations. She currently teaches at Sarah Lawrence College.

Vinnie-Marie D'Ambrosio spent her childhood painting, writing, and putting on musical shows. Armed with various scholarships, she attended Smith College, where she studied American Culture. She has since made a home for herself and her daughter in a Brooklyn brownstone, and joined the English faculty at Brooklyn College. Her poetry has won two national awards, and she has published a volume of poems, *Life of Touching Mouths*. She is the founder and coordinator of the weekly poetry reading series, in its fourth year, at The Brooklyn Museum.

Diane Di Prima was born in 1934 in New York City and attended Swarthmore College. Her active involvement in contemporary poetry includes her work as editor of *The Floating Bear*, contributing editor of *Kulchur*, associate editor of *Signal Magazine*, and publisher and printer of The Poets Press. Her poetry includes *This Kind of Bird Flies Backward*, *Dinners and Nightmares*, *The New Handbook of Heaven*, *Poems for Freddie*, and *Revolutionary Letters*. She is the recipient of a grant from the National Institute of Arts and Letters.

Elaine Edelman was born in Minneapolis, grew up in Dallas, took her B.A. from Sarah Lawrence College, and now works in New York. A Fellow of The New Dramatists, Inc., her play *Mother of Pearl* was premiered by the Co. Theater of Los Angeles in 1973. Her poetry, published in a number of magazines, appears in *Young North American Poets* and in *Noeva: Three Women Poets*.

Mari E. Evans is the author of *I Am A Black Woman*, from which the selections in this anthology have been taken.

Mary Fabilli was born in Gardiner, New Mexico, in 1914 and studied at San Francisco State College and the University of California at Berkeley. She is the Associate Curator of History, Oakland Museum. Her volumes of poetry are *The Old Ones, Aurora Bligh and Early Poems*, and *The Animal Kingdom*. She cites the influences in her life as the Brontë sisters, Emily Dickinson, Teresa of Avila, Catherine of Siena, Charles Dickens, Don Marquis, and Bruno Barilli.

Gena Ford is a Northwest poet from Portland, Oregon, and advisory editor to The Elizabeth Press, which has published her books. These include *Tall Tales for Far Courses, A Planting of Chives*, and *Poems 1964-67*. Her work has also been published in *West Coast Review, Northwest Review*, and *St. Andrew's Review*.

Gail Fox was born in the United States in 1942, but is now a Canadian citizen. She received her B.A. from Cornell University in 1964, has two children, and is separated from her husband. The author of five books of poetry including *God's Odd Look*, she is presently working on a long prose-poem to be published in 1976. Of herself, she writes, "I am a woman, I suffered, I was there."

Kathleen Fraser was born in 1937 in Tulsa, Oklahoma, and received her B.A. from Occidental College. Her work was included in the first *Young American Poets* anthology edited by Paul Carroll, and she won the Dylan Thomas Poetry Award from the New School in 1967. She has taught at San Francisco State College, the University of Iowa, and Reed College. Her volumes of poetry include *Change of Address, In Defiance of the Rains*, and *Little Notes to You from Lucas Street*. She was married for eight years to the poet and novelist Jack Marshall and has one son.

Elsa Gidlow was born December 29, 1898, in Yorkshire, England. Her childhood was spent in Canada and New York City. Since 1926 she has lived in the San Francisco Bay area, earning her living as editor, writer, journalist. A feminist since the age of fourteen, when she gave up her formal schooling, she has written one book of verse and five poetry pamphlets. A volume of her Lesbian love poetry, *Sapphic Songs, Seventeen to Seventy*, is forthcoming.

Virginia Gilbert has taught creative writing at the University of Utah. Her poetry has been published in *North American Review*, *New Voices in American Poetry*, *Prairie Schooner*, and *Beloit Poetry Journal*.

Nikki Giovanni comes from Lincoln Heights, Ohio. At sixteen she entered Fisk University, where she studied writing with John Killens and edited the campus literary magazine. On returning to the Cincinnati area, she initiated an awareness of arts and culture in the black community. Her books are *Black Feeling, Black Talk, Black Judgment*, *Gemini*, *Re: Creation*, and *Night Comes Softly*. She is now living in New York and is on the staff of Rutgers' Livingston College.

Mary Gordon has been published in *The Little Magazine*.

Geraldine Hammond, a professor of English at Wichita State University, has had poems and articles published in various journals. She obtained her Ph.D. from the University of Colorado, and received the First Regents Award for Excellence of Teaching in 1966. She wrote the poetry for a musical performance by chorus and orchestra of a commissioned work titled *Wheatland*, and a long poem for choric reading, *It Must Be Said*, which has been performed by several groups.

Jeanine Hathaway was born in Chicago in 1945. She was a member of the Sisters of St. Dominic (Adrian, Michigan) for nine years, and as such, taught in elementary schools in Detroit, Toledo, and Cleveland. In 1973 she received an M.F.A. from Bowling Green State University. She currently lives in Wichita, Kansas, with fiction writer/husband Stephen; both of them teach creative writing at Wichita State University.

Anne Hazlewood-Brady is the author of four books of poetry. The latest, *The Cross, the Anchor & the Heart*, was published in 1975. She is currently a member of the Arts and Humanities Commission of Maine, where she lives. As an ardent feminist she served on the committees which organized the Women's Strike and Women's March in New York City, 1970-71, and was a founder of the Women's Center and Women's Interart Center.

Margery Himel has been published in *Moving Out*.

Lindy Hough is the author of *Changing Woman*, *Psyche* and *The Sun in Cancer*, all collections of poems. She is coeditor and publisher of *Io*, with Richard Grossinger, and has taught writing, literature, and women's studies at Eastern Michigan University, the University of

Maine at Portland-Gorham, and Goddard College. She lives in Plainfield, Vermont, and is working on a forthcoming novel called *Cruel and Imperfect Strangers*.

Barbara Howes was born in 1914 in New York City and now makes her home in North Pownal, Vermont. A graduate of Bennington College, her honors include a Guggenheim Fellowship, a Brandeis University Creative Arts Poetry Grant, and the Award in Literature from the National Institute of Arts and Letters. Her books of poems include *The Undersea Farmer*, *In the Cold Country*, *Light and Dark*, *Looking Up at Leaves*, and *The Blue Garden*. She is also the editor of *Twenty-three Modern Short Stories*, *From the Green Antilles*, and *The Eye of the Heart: Short Stories from Latin America*.

Colette Inez was born in Brussels, Belgium, and was brought up in a Catholic home for children. She came to the U.S. at the start of World War II and received her B.A. degree from Hunter College in 1961. Her work has appeared in numerous national and international poetry magazines and literary journals. Her collection, *The Woman Who Loved Worms*, received the 1972 Great Lakes Colleges Association National Book Award. Ms. Inez conducts a poetry workshop at the New School, New York City, and is among the 1975 recipients of fellowships from the National Endowment for the Arts and New York State CAPS (Creative Artists Public Service).

Phyllis Janik, born in Chicago in 1944, has an M.F.A. from the Iowa Writers' Workshop. She teaches at Moraine Valley College and works in the Illinois Poets in the Schools program. Her work has appeared in a variety of magazines and she has published a book of poems entitled *The Disaster Expert* and a chapbook entitled *Red Shoes*. She has one daughter.

Erica Jong was born in New York City in 1942. She studied at Barnard, Columbia Graduate Faculties and Columbia School of the Arts. Her works include two books of poetry, *Fruits & Vegetables* and *Half-Lives*, and a novel, *Fear of Flying*. She received *Poetry*'s Bess Hokin Prize and also a grant from the New York State Council on the Arts in 1971.

June Jordan was born in Harlem in 1936 and grew up in the Bedford-Stuyvesant section of Brooklyn. A poet and novelist, she maintains her commitment to positive, radical change through the black and women's movements. A new collection of poems, *New Days*, and a work on *Bessie Smith* are forthcoming. She is an assistant professor of English at City College in New York.

Suzanne Juhasz is an assistant professor of English at the University of Colorado, Boulder. She has published a chapbook of poems, *Love Affair*, and poems in many journals. Her critical books are *Naked and Fiery Forms: Modern American Poetry by Women*, *A New Tradition*, and *Metaphor and the Poetry of Williams, Pound, and Stevens*.

Hannah Kahn was born in New York City in 1911, and has lived in Miami, Florida, for the past thirty-seven years. Her one collection of poems, *Eve's Daughter*, has just gone into a third edition. She won the International Sonnet Competition from the Poetry Society of Great Britain and America, and for fifteen years was the poetry-review editor of the Miami *Herald*. Her poems have appeared in numerous magazines, and have been included in three of the *Borestone Mountain Best Poems* awards. Ms. Kahn has three children.

Faye Kicknosway was born in 1936 in Detroit and grew up in poverty. She began writing poetry in 1963 when a friend "sent back a letter scanned, saying, you are a poet. look into it. did. am. poetry changed my life. continues to do that." She has published three volumes of poetry, *O. You Can Walk on the Sky? Good.*, *Poem Tree*, and *A Man Is A Hook. Trouble.*, and three volumes are forthcoming.

Carolyn Kizer was born in Spokane, Washington, in 1925, and received her B.A. from Sarah Lawrence College twenty years later. She founded the poetry quarterly *Poetry Northwest*, and was the first Director of Literary Programs under the National Endowment for the Arts. She has taught poetry and creative writing at several colleges and universities, and writes fiction. Her volumes of poetry include *The Ungrateful Garden*, *Knock Upon Silence*, and *Midnight Was My Cry*.

Carol Konek teaches women's studies and freshman composition at Wichita State University. Coediting this anthology has been the most fulfilling educational experience of her life.

Mary Norbert Körte has been a participant of the California Poets in the Schools (PITS) program, and is interested in working with women's groups. Her volumes of poetry include *Hymn to the Gentle Sun* and *The Midnight Bridge*.

Maxine Kumin was born in Philadelphia and received a B.A. and M.A. from Radcliffe College. She has taught at the University of Massachusetts at Amherst, Tufts, Columbia, and Brandeis. Her fourth book of poems, *Up Country*, was awarded the Pulitzer Prize. Her most recent collection of poetry was *House, Bridge, Fountain, Gate*, and she has written four novels, the latest entitled *The Designated*

Heir. Ms. Kumin lives on a farm in New Hampshire, where she struggles to care for a large vegetable garden and three horses.

Jacqueline Lapidus grew up in New York City, lived in Greece for three years, then settled in Paris, where she works for a literary agency and is active in the women's movement. Her first book of poems was *Ready to Survive*, and she is currently preparing a second book, *Starting Over*. In collaboration with Nathalie Stern, she has also translated into French the Goldman anthology *Red Emma Speaks*.

Lynne Lawner graduated from Wellesley College in 1957, was a Henry Fellow at Newnham College, Cambridge, in 1957-58, and lived in Italy on a Fulbright grant from 1958-1960. Most of her time since 1963 has been spent in Rome. She has published two books of poems, *Wedding Night of a Nun* and *Triangle Dream*. She has also published many translations of Italian and French poetry. She is presently a Fellow of Villa I Tatti, the Harvard University Center for Italian Renaissance Studies in Italy.

Denise Levertov was born in London and moved to the United States in 1948. Educated at home, the only school she attended was for ballet. Her first book was *The Double Image*; more recent works include *The Poet in the World* and *The Freeing of the Dust*. Ms. Levertov currently lives in Somerville, Massachusetts, and teaches at Tufts University.

Sharon Mayer Libera was born in St. Louis, Missouri, in 1944. She attended St. Louis University as an undergraduate and spent a year in England as a Fulbright Fellow at the University of Manchester. As a doctoral student in English at Harvard, she wrote her thesis on Ezra Pound. Since 1971 she has been an assistant professor of English at Mount Holyoke College. Her published writing includes poems, articles, and reviews.

Lyn Lifshin grew up in Middlebury, Vermont, and began writing poetry at an early age. She has given many readings and has had a large number of poems published in small magazines and anthologies. Her books of poetry include *Black Apples*, *Merchurochrome Sun Poems*, *I'd Be Jeanne Moreau*, *The Blue Cabin and Other Winter Fruit*, *Collected Poems*, *Poems*, *Love Poems*, *Upstate Madonna*, *The Old House*, *Plymouth*, *The Old House on the Croton*, *Other Houses*, *North*, *Plymouth Women*, and *Thru Blue Dust, New Mexico*.

Judith McCombs' first book, *Sister & Other Selves*, has just been published by The Glass Bell Press of Detroit. Her poems appear widely in little and feminist magazines here and in Canada, including *Poetry*,

Loon, Poetry Northwest, Fiddlehead, Waves, Aphra, and *Moving Out,* which Ms. McCombs co-founded in 1971. It is the nation's oldest surviving feminist literary arts magazine. She teaches literature and creative writing at the Center for Creative Studies, a Detroit college of art and design.

Susan MacDonald was born and educated in London and now lives in Menlo Park, California, with her two children. She has edited an anthology of women poets of the nineteenth and twentieth centuries. Of her creative efforts she writes, "Poetry is the song in all of us and serves the same purpose as a smile between strangers. When it's good it defines and distills something we always knew was there."

Naomi Long Madgett has lived in Michigan since 1946. She is the author of four volumes of poetry: *Songs to a Phantom Nightingale, One and the Many, Star by Star,* and *Pink Ladies in the Afternoon.* Her poems have been widely anthologized in this country and abroad. Ms. Madgett is a professor of English at Eastern Michigan University in Ypsilanti as well as editor/publisher of Lotus Press in Detroit. She is married and has a grown daughter, also a poet.

Carolyn Maisel grew up in East Texas, lived in Saudi Arabia and Spain, and took her creative writing degree at the Iowa Writers' Workshop. She is an editor of *Best Friends,* a women's poetry magazine located in Albuquerque, New Mexico, where she currently lives.

Ann Menebroker was born in Washington, D.C., in 1936 but has lived in California for many years. She has published four volumes of poetry, and her poems have been appearing in poetry magazines across the country for nearly twenty years. She is currently the coeditor of *Wine Rings,* and is doing review work for a poetry magazine. One of several anthologies her work has appeared in, *Six Poets,* was a Small Press Book Club selection.

Eve Merriam's first book won the Yale Younger Poets Award; subsequent volumes include *The Inner City Mother Goose, The Nixon Poems, The Double Bed,* and *A Husband's Notes About Her.* She is also the editor of *Growing Up Female in America: Ten Lives,* which has been dramatized into the current theatrical work *Out of Our Fathers' House.* Ms. Merriam was born in 1916 in Philadelphia and currently lives in Stonington, Connecticut.

Josephine Miles was born in 1911 in Illinois. She is now living in Berkeley, where she has been teaching at the University of California since 1940. She is the author of a number of books of literary history and poetry. The most recent are *Poetry and Change* and *To All Appearances*. Her work has appeared in many anthologies, and she was one of the California poets to be recorded on *Today's Poets II*. She has received an award from the National Institute of Arts and Letters, and won the Blumenthal Award from *Poetry*.

Vassar Miller was born in 1924 in Houston, Texas, and received her B.A. and M.A. degrees from the University of Houston. She has traveled over much of the United States and in Europe, and is presently living in Houston, where she has conducted tutorial courses in creative writing at St. John's School. Her books of poetry include *Adam's Footprint*, *Wage War on Silence*, which was nominated for the Pulitzer Prize, *My Bones Being Wiser*, and *Onions and Roses*.

Barbara Moraff lives in Dairyhill, South Royalton, Vermont. A coffeehouse poet in the fifties, her work was published in *Blue Beat* and other magazines of the time. She lived for a while in the Cherry Valley-Woodstock neighborhood of Vermont, a favored gathering place of poets for many years. Ms. Moraff was one of the poets included in *Four Young Lady Poets*.

Robin Morgan's first book of poems was *Mónster*; her second is entitled *Lady of the Beasts*. She also compiled and edited *Sisterhood Is Powerful, the First Anthology of Writings from the Women's Movement*, and was poetry editor for *The New Woman*. A compilation of her essays on feminism from the early 1960's to the present entitled *Going Too Far* is forthcoming.

Lisel Mueller, born in Germany, has lived in the United States since the age of fifteen. She now resides in a wooded area near Chicago with her family. Of her poetry, she writes, "Many poems are responses to the accidents in our lives which become history or fate. Ideally, I would write poems that are both simple and sensuous." Her books include *Dependencies*, *Life of a Queen* (chapbook), and *The Private Life*, which was the Lamont Poetry Selection for 1975.

Deborah Munro was born November 19, 1947, in Toronto and has "been wandering about ever since." She is currently engaged in American Studies at the University of New Mexico—"a happy combination of love and discipline"—while working on a play. Her poems have been published in *Descant*, *Egg*, *Best Friends*, *Plus*, and *Haiku Magazine*.

Kathleen Norris moved to South Dakota in 1974, having worked in New York City for five years. "I am still a New Yorker (once it's in the blood it stays) but love the spare, hard landscape of the prairie. My mother's parents lived here for over fifty years: it feels like home. The move changed my writing. The poems in my second manuscript, tentatively titled 'Inheritance,' are much less wordy and diffuse than my early work." Her first collection is *Falling Off*.

Joyce Carol Oates was born in New York in 1938 and is currently associate professor at the University of Windsor, Ontario. She has published numerous collections of short stories, including *By the North Gate* and *The Wheel of Love*. Her novel *Them* won the National Book Award, and *A Garden of Earthly Delights* won an award from the National Institute of Arts and Letters. Her books of poetry are *Anonymous Sins and Other Poems* and *Love and Its Derangements*. A novel published in 1976, entitled *The Assassins*, is her twenty-fourth book.

Gloria Oden has held a John Hay Whitney Fellowship for creative writing. Her poems have been published in many magazines, including *The Saturday Review* and *Poetry Digest*, and in several American and German anthologies. She was also featured, along with May Swenson, in the Media Plus series *Poetry Is Alive & Well & Living in America*.

Ellen Pearce was born in New York City in 1946 and received a B.A. in English from Lake Erie College, Painesville, Ohio. She has traveled in Holland, Austria, Switzerland, and England. She has published one volume of poetry, *Live in (very) Minor Works*. About her work, she writes, "I do not strive to employ as many poetic devices as possible, with the result that I use almost none at all. My poems deal mostly with love situations, but to label them love poems would be inaccurate and an insult."

Marge Piercy was born in Detroit in 1936 and now lives in Wellfleet, Massachusetts. She has published four volumes of poetry: *Breaking Camp*, *Hard Loving*, *To Be of Use*, and *Living in the Open*. She is also included in a book with three other poets, *4-Telling*, and is the author of four novels: *Going Down Fast*, *Dance the Eagle to Sleep*, *Small Changes*, and *Woman on the Edge of Time*.

Sylvia Plath was born in Boston in 1932 and lived in Devonshire, England, with her children and husband, poet Ted Hughes, until her death at the age of thirty. While still a student at Smith College she won the Mademoiselle College Fiction Contest. After attending Cambridge University on a Fulbright grant, she taught at Smith. She won a number of prizes for her poetry, including *Poetry*'s Bess Hokin Prize and the first prize at the Cheltenham Festival in England in 1961.

Nancy Price is the author of a novel entitled *A Natural Death* and is now completing a novel about a woman who has never been trained to be a woman. Her poems have appeared in *The Saturday Review*, *The Atlantic Monthly*, *The Nation*, and *The Quarterly Review of Literature*, while her stories have appeared in *The Virginia Quarterly Review*. The mother of three college-age children and a former university teacher, Ms. Price presently lives in Cedar Falls, Iowa.

Paula Reingold has been published in *ETC*.

Adrienne Rich was born in Baltimore, May 16, 1929. Her first book won the Yale Younger Poets Award, and she traveled abroad on a Guggenheim Fellowship in 1952-53. She married the economist Alfred Conrad and spent the next thirteen years raising three sons. A second Guggenheim in 1962 sent her to Holland. In 1966 she began teaching poetry workshops at Swarthmore and Columbia, then basic writing in the SEEK program at City College, where she remained. Of her six books, four are in print, the most recent being *Poems, Selected and New, 1950-1974*. Her prose book on motherhood is forthcoming.

Muriel Rukeyser was born in 1913 in New York City. She is the author of ten books of poetry, four books of prose, several children's books, and translations of Octavio Paz and Gunnar Ekelof. She holds the Swedish Academy Translation Award and many of America's top prizes for poetry. She is a member of the National Institute of Arts and Letters, the Society of American Historians, and the History of Science Society. Her latest volumes of poetry are *The Speed of Darkness*, *Waterlily Fire*, and *Breaking Open*.

Sonia Sanchez was born in Birmingham, Alabama, in 1935. Volumes of her poetry include *Homecoming*, *We a BaddDDD People*, and *It's a New Day*, all published by Broadside Press. Her poems have appeared in *Negro Digest*, *Liberator*, *Journal of blk/poetry*, *Soulbook*, *Nommo*, *blk/scholar*, and in *Broadside Series*. Her plays include *The Bronx Is Next* and *Dirty Hands*. She has taught at Manhattan Community College and the University of Massachusetts at Amherst.

Helga Sandburg was born in 1918 in Maywood, Illinois, and often served as secretary for her father, writer/poet Carl Sandburg. She has written six novels, two books of nonfiction, three children's books, and two volumes of poetry, *The Unicorns* and *To a New Husband*. Her short stories, individual poems, and articles have been published in many national magazines including the *New Yorker*, *Harper's*, *The Saturday Review*, and women's magazines. Ms. Sandburg has won many prizes for her short stories and poetry, and currently lives in Cleveland, Ohio.

Susan Fromberg Schaeffer is a professor of English at Brooklyn College. Her books of poetry are *The Witch and the Weather Report*, *Granite Lady* (which was a National Book Award nominee), and *Rhymes and Runes of the Toad*. Her novels include *Falling* and *Anya*. She is currently at work on a new novel, *Time In Its Flight*, and a new book of poems.

Anne Sexton was born in 1928 in Newton, Massachusetts. Her poems have appeared in virtually every important literary magazine in the United States and she was the recipient of numerous awards, fellowships, grants, and prizes. Her books of poetry are *To Bedlam and Part Way Back*, *All My Pretty Ones*, *Live or Die*, which won the Pulitzer Prize, *Love Poems*, *Transformations*, *The Book of Folly*, and *The Death Notebooks*. Anne Sexton died at her home in Weston, Massachusetts, in October 1974. She left several manuscripts that will appear posthumously, including a collection entitled *43 Mercy Street*.

Clarice Short was born in Kansas and grew up in the Ozarks of Arkansas. She received her B.A. and M.A. degrees from the University of Kansas, and her Ph.D. from Cornell University. From 1946 until her retirement in 1975, she taught at the University of Utah and pursued postdoctoral research at Harvard, Oxford, and London universities. She has published articles on various authors and aspects of literature of the Romantic and Victorian eras, as well as a collection of poems entitled *The Old One and the Wind*.

Anita Skeen, born in Charleston, West Virginia, has an M.F.A. from Bowling Green State University and taught there for a year before taking a position at Wichita State University. Her poetry has appeared in *Nimrod*, *Quartet*, *Kansas Quarterly*, *The Greenfield Review*, *New Letters*, and anthologies such as *Itinerary II: Poetry* and the *Three Mountains Press Anthology of Poetry*.

Helen Sorrells' first collection of poetry is *Seeds as They Fall*, although her poems have been published in many magazines and literary journals and have been included in the anthologies *The Women Poets in English*, *The Borestone Mountain Best Poems of 1967*, *Poets West*, *The*

Girl in the Black Raincoat, and *Moving to Antarctica*. In 1973 she was given a creative writing grant by the National Endowment for the Arts.

Kathleen Spivack is the author of two books of poetry, *Flying Inland* and *The Jane Poems*. Her work has received wide attention and she has won prizes and national recognition. She has been published in numerous anthologies and in national and international magazines as well as in small-press publications. Ms. Spivack teaches the Advanced Poetry Workshop at the Radcliffe Graduate Center, Cambridge, Massachusetts, and is currently at work on a third volume of poems.

Ann Stanford has written five books of poetry as well as a verse translation of the *Bhagavad Gita*, an anthology called *The Women Poets in English*, and most recently a critical work, *Anne Bradstreet: The Worldly Puritan*. She has received the Award in Literature from the National Institute of Arts and Letters and the Shelley Memorial Award for distinction in poetry.

Lynn Strongin was born in 1939 in New York City. She was first published in *31 New American Poets*, and her work has appeared in numerous anthologies and periodicals. She has published two volumes of poetry, *The Dwarf Cycle* and *Shrift*. In 1972 she received a creative writing grant from the National Endowment for the Arts, and is now finishing a dissertation, "Six Women Poets," under a grant from the American Association of University Women.

May Swenson was born in 1919 in Logan, Utah, and moved to New York City shortly after she earned a bachelor's degree from Utah State University. She has written seven books of poetry, including two volumes for young readers. Four of her books have been leading contenders for the National Book Award, a number of her poems have been set to music, and her poetry is included in nearly fifty noteworthy anthologies. She has enjoyed a number of grants and prizes, and is particularly proud of her membership in the National Institute of Arts and Letters. At present she is in the process of assembling her *New and Collected Poems*.

Velma West Sykes spent most of her adult life in Kansas City, free-lancing poetry, feature articles, and book reviews for the *Kansas City Star*, *Saturday Evening Post*, *Kansas Quarterly*, *Christian Century*, *Denver Post*, and many other publications, as well as the Associated Press. On local WDAF she was the voice of "The Gentle Reader," a poetry program. Retiring from her editorial position on *Boxoffice Magazine* to live in Fort Collins, she is now director of the Fort Collins Workshop of the Poetry Society of Colorado.

276

Constance Urdang was born and brought up in New York City. Since leaving there, she has lived in the Midwest, New England, and Mexico. Married to poet Donald Finkel, she and her husband have two daughters and a son. Her first book of poems, *Charades + Celebrations*, was published in 1965. A novel, *Natural History*, followed in 1969. Another volume of poetry, *The Picnic in the Cemetery*, was published in 1975.

Mona Van Duyn was born and grew up in Iowa, and began writing poems in the second grade. She studied at the Iowa Writers' Workshop and taught writing and literature in universities for twenty-three years. At present she lives in St. Louis, Missouri, with her husband, Jarvis Thurston, and travels about the country giving readings of her poetry. She has published five books of poems and has received many honors, including the Bollingen Prize and the National Book Award.

Julia Vinograd says of herself, "I was born in 1943, got my B.A. at Cal Berkeley and my M.F.A. at the University of Iowa. For the last 10 years I've been living in Berkeley, blowing soap bubbles and writing. I've got 7 small books out. I wear a yellow striped cap."

Diane Wakoski earns her living giving poetry readings on college campuses and is currently the Writer in Residence at Michigan State University. She has published nine collections of poems, the most recent being *Virtuoso Literature for Two and Four Hands*, and nine slim volumes of poetry. She does not believe that separating poetry into categories, such as women's poetry, black poetry, southern poetry, etc., is useful, and hopes that she is not read because she was born with certain unselected sexual characteristics.

Alice Walker was born in Georgia in 1944. Her collection of short stories, *In Love & Trouble*, won the Richard and Hinda Rosenthal Award of the National Institute of Arts and Letters, and her book of poems *Revolutionary Petunias* was nominated for a National Book Award. Other books include a novel, *The Third Life of Grange Copeland*, and a collection of poems, *Once*. She has received many awards for her work, and her essays have appeared in several national publications. Her new novel, *Meridian*, is forthcoming.

Kath Walker has published a volume of poetry entitled *We Are Going*.

Margaret Walker was born in 1915 in Birmingham, Alabama. She attended Northwestern University and received her M.A. from the University of Iowa. She has taught at Livingstone College and Jackson State College and has worked also as a typist, reporter, and editor.

Among her awards are the Yale Younger Poets Award for *For My People* and the Houghton Mifflin Literary Fellowship for her novel, *Jubilee*. Her most recent volume of poetry is *Prophets for a new day*.

Dorothy Walters teaches classes in women's literature at Wichita State University, where she is associate professor of English and coordinator of women's studies. She is the author of *Flannery O'Connor* in the Twayne United States Authors Series. In her spare time, she studies metaphysics and the poetic imagination.

Ruth Whitman was born in 1922. She has received several awards and was a Fellow in Translation and Poetry at the Radcliffe Institute for two years. Her books include *Blood & Milk Poems*, *The Passion of Lizzie Borden: New and Selected Poems*, and *The Marriage Wig*. She is the editor and translator of *An Anthology of Modern Yiddish Poetry*, and the editor of *The Selected Poems of Jacob Glatstein*.

Nancy Willard teaches in the English department at Vassar College and lives in Poughkeepsie with her husband and four-year-old son. Earlier poetry collections include *Skin of Grace* (winner of the Devins Memorial Award for 1967), *19 Masks for a Naked Poet*, and *Carpenter of the Sun*, and she has published a collection of stories, *Childhood of the Magician*. She has also written four books for children.

Sarah Youngblood was born in Tyrone, Oklahoma, and has made her living as a teacher, first at the University of Minnesota and now at Mount Holyoke College. She writes of herself, "I make my life, if not my living, as a poet and a carpenter. I count myself triply blessed: to be alive, to carry poems in my head, to have seen the sea."

INDEX OF TITLES

INDEX OF POETS

INDEX OF FIRST LINES

COPYRIGHT
ACKNOWLEDGMENTS

No. 2, reprinted by permission of *Amazon Quarterly* and the author.

LYNNE LAWNER: "Rino's Song," from *Triangle Dream and Other Poems* by Lynne Lawner, copyright © 1969 by Lynne Lawner, reprinted by permission of Harper & Row, Publishers, Inc.

DENISE LEVERTOV: "Bedtime," and "The Mutes," from Denise Levertov, *The Sorrow Dance*, copyright © 1966 by Denise Levertov Goodman, reprinted by permission of New Directions Publishing Corp.; "Matins," and "Sunday Afternoon," from Denise Levertov Goodman, reprinted by permission of New Directions Publishing Corp.

SHARON MAYER LIBERA: "Mother," and "Patty, 1949-1961," printed by permission of the author.

LYN LIFSHIN: "Even There," and "In Spite of His Dangling Pronoun," from *Black Apples* by Lyn Lifshin, reprinted by permission of The Crossing Press.

JUDITH MCCOMBS: "The Dictionary Is an *Historian*," from *Moving Out*, Vol. 2, No. 1, reprinted by permission of Wayne State University Press.

SUSAN MACDONALD: "The Children," from *Ms.*, July 1972, reprinted by permission of *Ms. Magazine*, copyright © 1972 by *Ms. Magazine* Corp.

NAOMI LONG MADGETT: "Her Story," from *Star by Star* by Naomi Long Madgett, Detroit, Harlo Press, 1965, 1970, reprinted by permission of the author.

CAROLYN MAISEL: "A Dream of Women," printed by permission of the author; "A Letter from a Friend," from *Best Friends*, and "The Girl in the Willow Tree," from *The North American Review*, both reprinted by permission of the author.

ANN MENEBROKER: "To the Man I Live With," from *It Isn't Everything*, copyright © 1968 by Ann Menebroker 4, reprinted by permission of the author.

EVE MERRIAM: "The Fertile Valley of the Nile," from *The Double Bed* by Eve Merriam, copyright © 1958, 1972 by Eve Merriam, reprinted by permission of M. Evans & Co., Inc., New York, New York 10017.

JOSEPHINE MILES: "I've been going around everywhere," from *Kinds of Affection*, copyright © 1964 by Josephine Miles, reprinted by permission of Wesleyan University Press.

VASSAR MILLER: "On Approaching My Birthday," copyright © 1968 by Vassar Miller, from *Onions and Roses* by Vassar Miller, reprinted by permission of Wesleyan University Press, "Reciprocity,"